CONFESSIONS OF A

Cutthroat Trout

Reflections on a Life of Adventure and Foolishness —and, by God's Grace, Service to Christ

ERIC E. ENGLEMAN

innovo
PUBLISHING
innovopublishing.com

Published by Innovo Publishing, LLC
www.innovopublishing.com
1-888-546-2111

innovo
PUBLISHING
innovopublishing.com

Publishing quality books, eBooks, audiobooks, music, screenplays & courses for the Christian & wholesome markets since 2008.

CONFESSIONS OF A CUTTHROAT TROUT
Reflections on a Life of Adventure and Foolishness—and, by God's Grace, Service to Christ

Library of Congress Control Number: 2024911295
ISBN: 979-8-88928-026-2

Cover Design & Interior Layout: Innovo Publishing, LLC

Printed in the United States of America
US Printing History
First Edition: 2024

Has God called you to create a Christ-centered or wholesome book, eBook, audiobook, music album, screenplay, or online course? Visit Innovo's educational center (cpportal.com) to learn how to accomplish your calling with excellence.

CONTENTS

PREFACE

D ear reader, thank you for having an interest in my life story. I really hope that it will be a blessing to you and that you will find it a pleasure to read. Being not a publicly-known figure nor the leader of a great social media following, one might ask why I would write such a "memoir." As I wrote several other books in the last few years, I came to see that I could write well enough, and, more importantly, I came to a fuller realization just how spectacularly good God has been to me. So I figured that I could combine these and produce something that might very well interest and encourage people.

There is a temptation in autobiographies to make the writer glow a bit more than what was the case. Here, I've tried to recount things (in chronological order) as they really were, warts and all. Well, not all the *warts*, but enough to show that my inner character and outward behavior fell "short of the glory of God." In the process I was not always faithful or kind to my fellow man. Enough is included here such that I might find some discredit in the eyes of some; but I ask such readers to hang in there with me because the *discredit* will by and by show all the more the amazing grace God has manifested in my life.

Growing up in lumberjack country, being an adventurer at heart, and having been a sailor ranging five of the seven seas, a few tall tales—but honestly told—have crept into the book. Some may find these entertaining, but others of a more dainty constitution may react with a gentle gasp. Again, I ask these to press on—skipping bits here and there if necessary—recalling that "Christ Jesus came into the world to save sinners" (1 Timothy 1:15). The seas will become calmer the closer the autobiographical ship gets to safe harbor.

No need for giving thanks here, for the people whom I owe thanks to are mentioned in loving ways in the book. One exception is Rick "Super Hunky" Sieman (d. 2023) whose columns at *Dirt Bike Magazine* were an inspiration for storytelling. Of course, I praise God who gave me my life, who redeemed me—through the offering up of His Son, Jesus—from the final judgment to come, and who gave me the blessed life depicted here. I dedicate the book to Captain Eric "Rico" Tibbets USN (Ret.), a fellow shipmate and aviator, who more than others led me to this awesome God.

—Eric E. Engleman
Apple Valley, California

PART ONE

Living for Me

1

Sinful, Slothful, and "Abnormal" from the Start

How shall the story begin? *I was born in 1958 at Bethesda Naval Hospital, Maryland, right next to Washington, DC.* Hmm, nope, let's start the story a bit earlier than that. My mother's maiden name was Earle, so, going back generations, her roots were mainly English, probably some French, in which there must have been an Earle or a Duke or maybe an Earle of Duke. On my father's side, which I know more about, Simon Engleman came with his brother Jacob from somewhere in the German-speaking world about the time of the War of Independence. There is some chance that Simon offered himself to public service once in the new world in view of the fact that he obtained a valuable land warrant applicable to a sizable section of rolling hills in Kentucky County, Virginia. The warrant was signed by no less than Governor Patrick Henry ("Give me liberty or give me death!"). Simon, along with Daniel Boone and others, were some of the first European settlers in that wild land. The records show that Simon fought Indians under the command of Colonel Logan, was deputized to enforce the law, profited from the first production of

Kentucky whiskey, and in time was the master of a large tobacco and corn plantation.

When he died in 1829, much of plantation life was auctioned off, first dibs going to family. Items of note in the estate sale were sections of land, many farm implements and animals, five whiskey producing stills, 195 barrels of whiskey, Dutch (German) Bibles, a six-volume set of Josephus (Jewish influence?), and about twenty slaves. Regarding this last category, Simon's son Christian transferred several of the oldest slaves into his domain—ages about sixty—where they probably remained for the rest of their lives. Christian was a devout Christian man and the executor of his father's estate, and one senses from the records that his taking on of the slaves just mentioned was a decision not based on business but on familiarity and compassion.

Christian inherited some of the land and sired sixteen children. His son Christian (II) moved to Missouri, where little is known of him, but it seems he was a relatively poor farmer and had a hand in forming one of the first churches there. He also had a son named Christian (III) who, when of age, moved to Vancouver, Washington, where he married a beautiful lady, Olivia, whose parents had emigrated from Sweden. Christian (III) turned out to be a creative and enterprising young man: he opened the first (silent) movie theater in Vancouver (in the upstairs room above his billiard parlor) and designed and patented the first mechanical billiard player! His firstborn, again, Christian (IV), was born in 1906 in the theater building, but when he was about ten his mother died in the influenza pandemic that ravaged America and Europe during and just after the First World War.

This last Christian—"Chrissy," as he was called then, my father—was a mischievous yet brilliant lad. In his early teens he made his own wireless radio set, tied illegally into the local power grid (causing city lights to brown out at night, which got him into some trouble), and communicated with early "hams" all over the Northwest. One day a Coast Guard cutter that needed a radio operator came into port, and when it left a few days later, Chrissy was onboard—with his dad's worried permission and his age rounded up to meet the need.

While with that ship, Dad had all kinds of adventures, both underway and ashore. As to the former, he heard a "Mayday" call from a ship in distress and was able to figure out a bearing using his wireless knowhow. The sinking ship was found and the crew saved. As to the latter, at one port o' call in south Alaska the sailors were invited to a dance hall where local ladies had gathered to meet the boys. A large coastal Indian woman took possession of my dad and kept him as a dance partner the whole night, flinging him around the floor. When the party ended, she declared, "Now we go to my house, and we drink salmonberry wine." Dad courteously declined and got out of there and back to the ship as fast as he could. These sort of events portended events in the life of his son many years later.

My father was so good at what he did in the Coast Guard that they recommended him to the Naval Academy (Annapolis, Maryland). So in 1926 that's where he went, and that's where he excelled at all things academic and athletic. Upon graduating with the class of 1930, he at first pursued the new (and extremely dangerous) warfare specialty path of naval aviation, but medical issues put him back on the track that he'd been on through his academy education— i.e., electrical engineering and the research and development that flowed from it. In this, Dad excelled (and *lived*, for many—maybe most—of his classmates in aviation lost their lives in accidents and the war) and went on to be at the cutting edge of radio, radar, sonar, and even atomic weapons R & D.

When I was a kid, Dad used to speak about how radar back in the day was so top secret that, as a code word, they spelled it backwards. And he was so intimately involved with the development of sonar that he was the one who came up with its name. Dad was even tangentially involved with the Manhattan Project, and when test bombs were exploded over Bikini Atoll in the South Pacific after the war, he commanded a research ship that studied the underwater flora and fauna before and after the tests. In the post-blast submarine hellscape, they discovered a new mutant fish, and that bizarre creature was named after my father (*Synodus englemani*). He confessed that at one test the forecast winds unexpectedly shifted, and the radioactive fallout fell on his ship and crew instead of elsewhere. Because of that,

13

doctors sternly warned him never to have children, lest they turn out terribly abnormal.

I and my brother, Mark, and sister, Katherine, are the product of our father's second marriage. His first marriage produced two children, Chris Jr. and Virginia. None of us have been great, but we haven't been flops either: Chris Jr., naval officer and pianist; Ginny, mother and photographer; Mark, naval officer and entrepreneur; Eric, naval officer and Christian minister/writer; and Katherine, naval officer, singer, and commercial real estate appraiser.

Some years after the divorce (from his first wife), Dad—by then retired (Captain) from the Navy but staying close to military R & D business in the Washington, DC, area—met our mother on an American Airlines flight (more portending) from Boston to Washington, DC. Mom was a stewardess on the flight and was impressed with how this dashing middle-aged man cared for the young unaccompanied girl next to him.

This man, who seems to be single, would make a wonderful match for my mother, she thought (her mother was also divorced). By the end of the flight, Mom had somehow telegraphed an interest, so Dad suggested that she and her mother meet him for dinner that night at the posh "Pirates Cove" (or a name to that effect). Mom accepted, brought her mom, and met Dad at the restaurant, but by the end of the evening, Mom had decided—despite their twenty-four-year difference in age—to keep him for herself. That she did, in loving matrimony, for almost forty years until Dad died in 1995.

OK, now back to *I was born.* Because Dad was still in the military consulting business in 1958, and because he was a veteran, I was born on June 28th at Bethesda Naval Hospital near Washington, DC. The three children came one right after the other, so we had a woman named Evelyn who helped out—a woman who held a big place in my heart till her death many years later. By 1960 Dad was tired of the DC scene and wanted to return to his roots and raise his children there. A childhood buddy managed to find a timber farm with a big log house near Vancouver, Washington, for relatively little money, so "Kanati Falls Ranch" (so named by Mom) was bought and off we went to the mountainous and forested Pacific Northwest. Evelyn came too.

Because the stock market soon thereafter tanked and put Dad in a financial jam, we had to return to DC about a year later. My very first memory is from this time: in a kindergarten class I stole vanilla wafer cookies from the teacher and was sent home as a result—a sinner from the start! To this day I still haven't fully conquered the sin of cookie thievery. Two years later, Dad took a job with a company near Carmel Valley, California. There we rented a spacious house that overlooked the valley. Mark and I had fun exploring the surrounding area, but a greater desire—never fulfilled—was to explore the big mountains that were visible on the other side of the valley. And even more, I looked forward to the day when we would return to the ranch and adventure.

Just a few memories from Carmel Valley will do. This was 1964, and "flower children" were popping up. One was the daughter of our neighbors. Her name was Lindsay. I would visit their home and sit at her feet as she took her guitar and played "Where Have All the Flowers Gone?" and "Turn! Turn! Turn!" and "Blowin' in the Wind," and I'd gaze at her beflowered brown hair draped across her shoulders and marvel how much her voice sounded like a beautiful songbird. I was six, and she was fifteen, yet I was completely in love with her. I would have sailed my entire Navy for her if I'd had one, but alas, I had nothing to offer except adolescent secret admiration.

On the other hand, at that time, I apparently had no feelings for the One who would one distant day be my Lord and Savior. In the public school Christmas play, I, a first grader and knowing little about Christ, played Joseph. After Jesus was born, and standing next to Mary as she held the child, I was supposed to kiss the plastic baby. But I just couldn't make myself do it despite repeated demands from the director. I don't know why.

One other memory: One day I got sick, and as the cold got better, Dad took me to get the toy of my choice. There on the wall was a plastic train locomotive and a plastic airplane. I really wanted the airplane, but I was too embarrassed to ask for it. So I chose the locomotive. That same feeling of embarrassment regarding airplanes would recur now and again, even up to the final steps of becoming a naval aviator nearly two decades later.

When I was seven, we moved back to the ranch for good. Right from the start, there was something of the Wild West and mountain man spirit in me, so after Dad gave me some initial lessons on fishing and how not to get lost, I was off and running. For me, it was a difficult paradise to grow up in: *difficult* in that our near two hundred acres was in a treacherous canyon, the land was heavily forested and entangled with bushes and brush of endless variety, and all that was more often than not wet and muddy and slippery and cold; *paradise* in that the exploring and fishing opportunities were unending. We were on the edge of civilization, beyond us only forests and mountains and rivers and creeks. So growing up there, Mark was mainly into stamp collecting, rock hounding, playing sports, and taking care of the few cattle. Katherine was into reading, helping Mom domestically, tending her horses, and going on horseback to visit friends. But I fished and explored the untamed wilderness and, when home, shepherded all the chickens and other fowl. Fishing and fowl were my main concerns, concerns that would spiritually foreshadow things that would eventually come.

During the grade school years, Dad's employment usually required him to drive to Portland, so he wouldn't return home till early evening. Mom ran the home full time, and I'm sure glad she did because she was always there with a meal or help or advice before we left for school and when we returned. The general situation allowed me after school and on weekends the freedom to explore and fish farther away from home than Mom and Dad were aware of. By the time I was about ten, I knew every creek within a couple miles of home and what kind of trout was in each. On the main river up- and downstream of the house, I knew every riffle and hole and the likelihood of catching steelhead (seagoing rainbow trout, averaging about seven pounds) in each. I'd tell Mom I was goin' fishin', and she'd say, "Don't get too far away." But I'd get farther away than I should have, if just for the reason that when exploring up a creek I always felt like the trout-filled hole from Shangri-La would surely be around the next bend. So I'd keep pressing upstream even as the sun was going down. Thus I'd sometimes get back home well after dark—Dad, home by that time, annoyed, and Mom, worried with dinner getting cold. But I'd partially make up for it with the stringer full of beautiful rainbow and/or cutthroat trout.

Because of this worry over my whereabouts, Dad decided one day to give me an outdoor orienteering and navigation test to see if I was really safe to be out there all alone. He put me on the floor of our International Harvester Scout with a blindfold on, and he, along with brother Mark, drove here and there for about an hour and, still blindfolded, let me out, escorted by Mark. Dad then drove off. The test was to see if I could get back home on my own, with Mark along to rescue me in case I failed. He was supposed to not say a word about how to do it. So once Dad was gone, I was led some distance away from the road and then allowed to unmask. We were in a thick forest on a steep hillside, but I could see a logged-off area through the trees uphill, so that's where I initially headed. Mark said, "Where are you going?" I replied, "Up to that clearcut to get a look around."

Once there, I was able to get up on a tall stump and see some distance. Immediately I recognized "Bob's Mountain" about six miles away and massive Mount Hood way beyond that, and I could see that in the forested canyon just below us was a creek I had fished many times. If we went down that watershed, we would eventually meet the main river and then could just follow the river down about a mile to home. So I got off the stump and headed downhill back in the forest on a southeast bearing. Mark, looking concerned, said, "Where are you going?" "Down to Jackson Creek," I replied as I jumped down the steep slope. Turns out Mark didn't exactly know where we were, so over the course of the next couple hours, I was able to lead him safely home. We even beat Dad home who had stopped on the way back at Mr. Greening's to share a game of Cribbage and glass of honey wine. When Dad pulled up in the Scout and found us there, he was amazed, somewhat relieved, and satisfied that, from that time on, I'd be fine fishing and exploring on my own.

I was so blessed, unlike many today, to be raised by a loving father and a loving mother. The modern feminist movement has talked many, maybe most, women into the notion that career is more meaningful than family. At root is the distrust of men and of God. Men to some extent deserve this; God doesn't. But then this results in men being distrustful of women, so fewer get married, and those that do often end up divorced. Statistics show that women were happier under the old paradigm. Well, Mom was very happy and felt totally secure even though we were never wealthy by American standards. We had the appearance of being rich because of the ranch, but Dad got it in a fire sale when apparently no one else wanted it. Otherwise, from the time that we came out West the second time, Dad held different business and entrepreneurial jobs that were necessary to make ends meet.

Mom—some called her *Fancy Nancy*—was a terrific cook. She and Dad became very conscious of *heath food*, and so our diet was unusually nutritious. For example, Mom bought wheat grain, ground it at home in a noisy device that looked like the Apollo Lunar Lander, and baked truly *whole wheat* bread with it. Delicious! Mom was skilled at bandaging every wound and finding the right remedy for every kind of malady. On Sundays she had us dress in our Sunday best and would pile us in the Scout and drive us down to the Christian Science (CS) church in Camas (sister city of Washougal, our hometown). There, I didn't understand too much of what Mary Baker Eddy taught (founder of CS), but I did benefit from the Bible stories read in Sunday school. Our usual teacher was a very gracious and patient lady named Mrs. Lehr. She used to call me "doubting Thomas."

Once in a blue moon, Dad would take us to a more regular church. He had a traditional appreciation for Christianity, but he seldom spoke about it. We did, however, always have the Ten Commandments hanging on the kitchen wall. One of those commandments was repeated on the side of the kitchen cookie jar: "Thou Shalt Not Steal." That one item alone routinely demonstrated to me the biblical truth that I would learn much later: "For all have sinned and fall short of the glory of God."

Apparently I had some rudimentary concept of God early on. My first memory of such occurred when I was about seven or eight. Coming out of the boys' room door, I fell off the porch into a stickily holly tree. After jumping up in a lot of pain, I looked up in the sky and shook my fist at God—my first spiritually sensitive moment. My next memory was perhaps a little more pleasing to my Maker and more indicative of where things would eventually go. On one of the rare occasions that Dad took us to church, I had an experience that moved me—but I don't recall the details, other than this: The church was somewhere up the nearby Columbia River gorge. It was a typical small church, and we were toward the back on the left side. I was sitting on the far right of the pew next to the aisle, I was emotional because of something that was said from the front of the church, and I started to raise my hand but was embarrassed that Dad might see me. That's it. Was it an "altar call"? I don't recall. Whatever it was, it didn't seem to have any lasting effect, although maybe it planted a seed that would sprout much later.

Dad loved us and was completely devoted to us, yet I somewhat feared him. The problem was that I was a dreamer, easily bored, and only interested in fishing and exploring and commiserating with the chickens. Oh, I should mention that I was lazy too. But Dad strongly stressed school and good grades and getting our many chores done on time. Thus I often failed to meet expectations. Mark, one year older, was stronger and far better at work and school. Katherine, one year younger, pretty much got straight A's. Back then it occurred to me that Mark was like the rainbow trout that I routinely caught: they struggled mightily when hooked and jumped like mad. On the other hand, I was more like the cutthroat trout that inhabited the smaller streams: they were shyer, weaker, and didn't fight near as hard. Yet I enjoyed fishing for the cutthroats more than the rainbows. So between Dad and industrious Mark and straight A Katherine, I constantly felt a bit deficient. But school bored me to no end—not because the work was too simple for me (it was usually too hard) but because I just wasn't interested. There were no disability excuses back then, but looking back now, I think I had them all!

Being bored was my usual mental state, unless I was exploring up some mountain stream, catching colorful cutthroats. Once my reading skills got pretty good, I also found excitement in reading war stories, especially stories of bomber and fighter combat (Toland's *The Flying Tigers* was my favorite). I didn't mind telling others about my fishing adventures, but I continued to be embarrassed about my interest in airplanes. One day I saw a package of small plastic fighter airplanes at a store in Washougal and wanted it bad. Just about every major WWII fighter was there! But I was scared to buy them, sure that people in the checkout line and the cashier would scoff and laugh at me. So I let them be.

On the last day of seventh grade—my last day at Cape Horn-Skye Elementary School—I threw a small smoke bomb under the playground merry-go-round, and the kiddies on it scattered. I had been in trouble (never bad) many times before and had always been given the choice of my parents being notified or simply dropping my trousers and receiving the "board of education" on the backside. The second option was always chosen. Better to get it over with quick. But this time they called my father right away and asked him to come get me. Dad told them to send me off on foot. So I started the long walk home, having a feeling of dread not so much because of the smoke bomb but because of the semester report card that I carried wherein was inscribed all *C*'s and *D*'s. Dad would not be happy. At the halfway point, I went cross country, and when I got home and faced Dad, it didn't go as badly as I had feared—but he was quite disappointed in me.

Junior and senior high school were more interesting, but I continued to lag my siblings and peers with lackluster performance in the classroom and in sports. Plus, now that we were bused to the big city of Washougal for school, the kids were more numerous and more aggressive and, in some cases, meaner. One ornery fellow named Larry was a big mouth, and I told him so, then he wanted to fight after school. We all met, but at the last moment I chickened out—a dishonor that smarts even today. It was only later that I learned that he was a good fighter, so I probably saved my teeth that day.

Feelings for the other sex started to faintly appear. Ironically, my first minor encounter of such was a girl named Pam who invited me behind the curtains of the empty auditorium stage and kissed me on the lips when I was twelve years old. Even today I faintly remember the feeling, but at that time I didn't have any idea what it was all about. I still didn't know that a girl's anatomy was different than a boy's. The junior high staff started occasionally playing the latest hits in the auditorium, and we could dance if we wanted to. A blonde-haired girl named Connie took an interest in me, and we danced a few times—American Bandstand style—but I was more perplexed than pleased by all this.

Mark and Katherine continued to excel academically and socially, and I performed average at best and in early high school accumulated friends who were more "friends of a feather." They were fun to be with but did not spur me on to greater things. Mark really did well in sports, especially in track and field (he could pole vault to the moon!) and in wrestling. I tried these as well as football, but I struggled. In the 440-meter run I did OK, but that was about it, so I quit track and field after the first year. Wrestling for the Washougal Panthers (for three-plus years) was especially hard. It was a grueling sport that was far better fitted for *rainbows* than *cutthroats*. So my freshman year I didn't win a match. Things subsequently somewhat improved, but I never came close to going to district let alone state competitions like Mark did. I must say, however, that in all that time I only got pinned once, and that by a championship wrestler from a bigger school who had oozing acne from head to toe. When we squared off I just didn't know where to grab him. So he grabbed me and had me on my back within seconds. Wouldn't you know that that was my only match that ever made the local paper, photo and all! I was also on the football team for a couple years, but I only played in JV games against Indian tribe teams and got knocked out so often that I figured that I'd better not do it anymore.

I know that I could have worked harder at sports, but I learned quickly that some are more naturally gifted than others. I worked endlessly, for example, on successfully performing a fireman's carry move against an opponent in wrestling but could never actually do one in competition. But Mark did them routinely, along with many other moves that I seemed to be incapable of. In all this, I had to persist against discouraging opposition, and that persistence I think helped me to persist in extremely demanding situations later in life.

During my sophomore year, I got my driving license and was allowed now and again to drive to school on my own. We still had the four-wheel drive Scout, and about that time Dad obtained a new International pickup truck to use in my brother's extra-curricular picnic table business as well as in the work related to the two travel trailer parks that Dad had recently acquired—one in Portland and one on the Oregon Coast. For some years I had already driven the Scout all over the property and sometimes a little beyond. But getting my license meant that I could explore and fish further into the mountains than I had hitherto done.

In addition to the love of fishing and exploring, I now added the love of driving machines into the wilderness, and anywhere else for that matter. During the summers I would work at the trailer parks. Twice a day my job was to pick up the trash (with the pickup) at all the travel trailer spaces and take it to the dump and clean the bathrooms. After work we'd go fishing in the nearby creeks and at night go back to the dump to shoot rats. At the coast, Dad even had a burger joint for a little while called the Hungry Whale, featuring the "Whale Burger." So I used to flip burgers there too. In any case, as long as I was near fishing and had a truck to drive, I was happy.

Fortunately, any future interest in non-alcoholic mood-altering substances was nipped in the bud one night on the coast when, after work at the trailer park, a twenty-something girl I met invited me to go to her place and smoke something called marijuana. I'd already had my first cigarette, so I figured this marijuana wouldn't be much different. Once there, we smoked some of that product, which, as best I recall, didn't do much for me. It seemed to do something for her, though. On the way home in her '68 Dodge Charger, she went way too fast around a long sweeping turn, flew off the road, and spun out and came to rest with a huge Douglas fir tree about one inch from my door on the passenger side. It was like God was there with a catcher's mitt. It wouldn't be the last time. When we flew off the road I thought I was a goner for sure. With that, I forever linked marijuana and drugs in general with danger and had nothing to do with them from then on. Unfortunately, alcohol was not included in this link, and, as we'll see down the road, it facilitated in me a lot of foolishness. An example immediately follows.

One weekend I stayed home alone, and the rest of the family went to Eastern Washington to attend Mark's state wrestling finals. Mistake #1: I should have gone to support my brother. Before leaving, Mom and Dad said sternly, "No parties!" That evening I invited over several of my friends, we drank lots of beer and perhaps strong drink, and late that night I drove one of my friends' cars at high speed down to the steel bridge store to get some more. I don't recall much of the drive because I was so inebriated, but I do recall hitting a hundred on the speedo on the straight before the store. On the way back, I bypassed home, drove at wild speeds further up the mountain, hit a corner too fast, and went flying off the road. A stump tore out parts of the drivetrain, so we all had to walk back to the ranch—about three miles—in the rain and mud. We could have gone off the road somewhere else and died. Not long before, the boys from a family not far from us had done something similar, split the station wagon in half when they hit a tree at high speed, and all were killed, one even decapitated. But someone was watching out for us that night, and I didn't deserve it.

We eventually got everyone home, and the damaged car too. Then, in sundry ways, I tried to cover up the story—first by making my friend whose car I damaged promise to tell his parents that he was driving, that he was not drinking, and that I had nothing to do with it. Then I carefully cleaned the house so there would not be a trace of mischief.

But I missed a beer bottle cap under the couch, and sure enough, Mom found it when they all got home. Then one thing led to another. I lied and denied any party activity. Meanwhile, the parents of my friend with the damaged car smelt a rat and leaned on him, and after a couple days he finally caved. He called me and told me such and said that his parents were going to call mine. At that point I realized the gig was up, but maybe I could still get ahead of the story. So I went to Mom and Dad's bedroom at bedtime and produced some fake tears and told them that my conscience had gotten the better of me and that I knew it was the right thing to come clean and confess and thereby honor my parents. For a few minutes, they appeared to buy my story, but when my friend's parents called, Dad quickly sized up the real situation and shook his head in disappointment and disgust.

The next day down in the basement, he said, "Eric, it will be a long time till I ever trust you again," or very similar words. I was crushed and embarrassed beyond saying. To make matters worse, Dad had all the parents of the party attenders come over in order to decide how this sort of thing should never happen again. My shame of the scheming destructive liar and of losing my father's confidence was intense. But it was a valuable lesson I never forgot.

Twelve years of primary and secondary education finally ended, and I successfully got my diploma. I don't know how I did it because I don't ever remember being interested in any of the classes. The only class I recall with some vividness was the senior class where we learned to type on old typewriters. The teacher was tough but effective. If she caught us looking down, she'd cover our hands so we couldn't see the keyboard! It's a skill that is very useful even unto this very moment!

Mark and Katherine succeeded too, Mark excelling with about a 3.5 grade point average, and Katherine achieving "Salutatorian" status with a GPA just a pinch shy of 4.0. I was the "anchor man" with a respectable 2.0 or so GPA, but I was happy, and Mom and Dad were proud of me—events of the last couple years notwithstanding. Heck, I was even student body president my last year, but don't read much into that. I had never been in the student government before but thought I could be somebody, so I went for it. My opponent had previously served faithfully and was far more deserving and qualified. But I would have someone drive our yellow International pickup around the school while I, standing in the pickup bed, would beat on a marching band base drum and yell out promises that I could in no wise keep (including the promise that I'd get the smokers a place to smoke pot). So I won, learning in the process that voters can indeed be manipulated. My presidential epitaph was written at year's end by my opponent who was on the yearbook staff: "It was a year of apathy."

Narcissistically, I tried for the same position when I went to Clark Community College the next year, but I didn't get far. At lunch hour all the candidates gave speeches. Mine was the last, and I thought I'd win the crowd over with what at first seemed like a sexist joke, but I had a delightful and innocent punchline. Problem was that I told the first part to the crowd, but when I got to the good part, the bell rung, everyone jumped up to go to class, and no one heard the punchline. The next day I discerned that every female at the school was hopping mad at me. So my goose was cooked. If they'd only heard the punchline! God made *me* the punchline, but for my good.

I should mention that before saying goodbye to Washougal High School, they gave us a lengthy battery of questions that would indicate what vocation we should take in life. When the results came back, I thought for me they might recommend *wilderness fishing guide* or *Antarctic explorer* or *fighter pilot*. To my surprise and annoyance, they deemed that I was best psychologically suited to be a *nurse*. That was the last thing I wanted to do, so I dismissed the advice and forgot about it. But maybe there was some wisp of wisdom there.

The year at Clark College ('76–'77) was interesting not so much because of classes but because of the freedom I had and the new friends I met. Dad let me borrow the Scout over that time, so I put a cheap cassette player in it and a couple of cheap speakers in coffee cans on the floors (they'd fall over in corners), and I rocked down the highway to the rock band Rush while carbon monoxide wafted in through rust cracks in the floor. Dad arranged for me to live with a distant relative from his side, "Aunt" Violet, who had long since been a widow and had an old but impeccably orderly house on the north side of Vancouver (WA). Aunt Violet was very good to me and fed me very well. She was a devoted Christian lady (Lutheran, as I recall) and allowed her Christian perspective to rub off on me a little bit during the year I was there.

Although I found school to be kind of a grind, I also found a friend, Chuck Kellogg, whom I discovered to be a kindred spirit, and we had all kinds of good times partying and fishing and exploring. His mom and sisters hosted me on many overnights up in the foothills north of town and were very hospitable. One morning there I got in the Scout to go to town but thought I'd better see if the family needed anything, so I went back inside. From there, something caught my eye through their big picture window. It was the Scout rolling down the mountain by itself. I'd forgot to set the parking brake. I tried running after it but to no avail. It took out about a quarter mile of fence, flew over a road, and came to earth squeezed between two alder trees. Because both doors had been left open, the trees rendered them no longer serviceable. That was not the end of the Scout, but close to it. Dad wasn't happy about it. When I look back at events like that, I'm kind of amazed how much patience Dad had with me. A year or so later, I would crash and total my mom's new VW Scirocco flying off a country road corner. Dad didn't chew me out then either, but he did cry when he saw the car, realizing how close I had come to being killed.

While at Clark, I also palled around with my old high school friend and Katherine's best friend, Jeanette. This lovely girl had a coastal Indian background and loved our family very much. Her concern regarding me was displayed, for example, in the way she would panic and be overwhelmed by nausea when watching me being turned into a pretzel at a wrestling match. She would go anywhere with me and bait hooks and clean out fish guts too. She was always cheerful. I should have then claimed her as my own, but I was too stupid. On the other hand, about this time I became quite interested in a beautiful girl named Holly who, along with her gracious and elegant mother, Margaret, had been friends of our family for many years. With her I felt I was reaching for the moon, so I did not exhibit the kind of confidence necessary to be found appealing; thus romance only briefly appeared. This relational pattern would be repeated many times in the future.

Speaking of risky activity, toward the end of that year at Clark, Dad's Harvard Business School buddy Bob Young invited me to go with him up Mount Saint Helens, which then rose to nearly ten thousand feet. Ropes and crampons and ice axes were necessary because of the steep glaciated slope. I had climbed many of the local mountains near the ranch, but this was scary. We made it to the top after about six hours, but I got a horrible sunburn on my face as a result. For the next few days I was confined to bed at Aunt Violet's with burn blisters and in much misery. Even worse, the mountain was so mad that we climbed her that she blew up two years later.

2

Flying the Coop

A t the end of the academic year at Clark, Dad, who was still financing things, was not happy with my so-so grades and lack of direction. So one day at the ranch he threw a brochure down on the living room table. It had a picture of a toyish-looking soldier on it and had written on the top, *The Citadel.* He said, "If I'm going to waste my money on you, this is where you're gonna go!" My late teenage rebellious spirit immediately arose, and I stubbornly declined. I didn't want anything to do with remedial military school. (Earlier I had, at Dad's instigation, gone to an interview concerning a possible Naval Academy nomination but had not bothered to change clothes after fishing earlier in the day. The interviewer questioned why I came to the interview with dried fish blood and salmon egg effluence on my shirt. I didn't get a nomination. Katherine, however, would get a nomination a year later.)

Not long after, Dad sweetened the deal by offering me a job at a new (franchised) company he was founding in Atlanta, Georgia. If I would help sell business directories for him there for a year, then he would pay my way through The Citadel (aka, The Military College of South Carolina). We flew there to take a look around. Then, that evening, Dad abruptly said, "I need a yes or no—you have five minutes to decide." So I gulped down a ton of rebellious pride, knowing that this would be the best for me, and agreed to the deal. He was elated and a day or two later flew me to The Citadel to have a look around. It was late summer, hot, muggy, and rainy. The first-year cadets wore gray ponchos, eyes downcast, walking silently through the steamy, rain-filled gutters, looking like ghosts. After the morning tour, my host laid out the schedule for the afternoon, but I told him I'd seen enough. I would be there next year whether I wanted to or not.

That year in Atlanta before The Citadel was quite an adventure. When Dad first took me there, I couldn't believe it: he let me pick out a new "company car"—a VW Scirocco. (Mom was so impressed with the car that she bought one herself back home. That's the one I demolished. At the end of my Atlanta time, she received *my* Scirocco and drove it for nearly twenty years.) Selling business directories was a grind, and I wasn't much good at it. But not long after I got there, I met a fellow who introduced me to river canoeing. Our first trips were on the relatively easy waters of the Chattahoochee River near Atlanta, but in time we took on wilder waters in northern Georgia and had many good times.

The next year I went to The Citadel. On the flight there, I met a girl who was just then matriculating at the not far away Converse College. I saw Carolyn off and on during the next four years and knew that she was a quality and, probably, Christian girl. But, wanting further adventures, I passed up on a woman whom God maybe intended to be the perfect wife for me right at the start.

The first year at The Citadel was difficult, with hazing (not hands on, but on-demand calisthenics) being a constant threat. My roommate during "knob" year was an African-American football scholarship fellow who was easygoing and introduced me to the finer musical tastes of psychedelic funk offered by bands such as Parliament and Funkadelic. One hot day, an upperclassman of his same race wracked me till I thought I would die. For some unknown reason, he really had it out for me and darn near did me in. When released back to my room in utter exhaustion, I slammed the door closed and screamed out a racial slur and curse in furious anger. Then I turned to fall into bed, and, to my horror, there was my roommate laying there in his upper bunk bed looking silently at me. I immediately lamented, "Oh, Hillary, I'm so sorry!" He rolled back over, waved his hand, and said, "Ah, don't worry about it," and that was that. I wish today that more people would have the grace of Hillary when it comes to racial matters. People are ruined today by saying far less than what I said that day. We had a good relationship that first year, but I didn't see him much because of his many football obligations.

Most of my classmates in "H Company" were good ol' southern boys, but there were cats and dogs (like me) from elsewhere. I found these "kind fine refined ... southern Citadel gentlemen" to be friendly fellows overall, and they readily accepted me, probably because I was more or less a country boy like them and was born to a southern belle. Several of them and their parents would host me on holidays and show me wonderful southern hospitality. Sophomore and junior years I roomed with the Virginian Heber Willis, who turned out to be an excellent roommate and friend. He too was an outdoorsman, so we had some fun adventures and campouts, and his family received me warmly.

During this time, I also took some of the fellows on canoeing trips up on the Chattooga River that straddles South Carolina and Georgia. This river is truly a wild and scenic river with lots of rapids and even waterfalls. On one occasion, four of us took on this river after it had rained hard for weeks. It turned out to be a trying and dangerous expedition. At one point, I capsized in a raging rapid and got stuck underwater in a hydraulic and almost drowned. The four of us were lucky to get out of there alive. On another, more fair-weathered trip, several of the Converse girls (not Carolyn) even joined us, and all had a delightful time.

Don Noonan was on this last canoe trip with the ladies. He was elevated to Hotel company commander our senior year. Perhaps the most perilous adventure of all was with him in his dilapidated Baja Bug, driving from Charleston to his home in Arizona. When there was a headwind, the gutless Bug would slow to a crawl, and the semi-trucks would come close to running over us. Once in Arizona, we tubed precariously down the Salt River, lost flashlight power while deep inside a cave, were pummeled by hail while camping on San Francisco Peak, and argued endlessly about subjects that came up. While there, I looked at a newspaper one morning and couldn't believe my eyes: Mt. Saint Helens was no more. Not only was most of the mountain gone but a wonderful area as well just north of it where I had hiked and fished many times. Later that summer I had planned to visit that area again with my old backpacking buddy and neighbor Pete Greening; alas, all that was now a wasteland. After The Citadel, Don flew bombers and then fighters for the Marine Corps. Learning to operate and survive in that Baja Bug probably prepared him well for flying dilapidated Marine aircraft.

At The Citadel, I really didn't have any solid idea what to study, so (today I don't recall why) I elected for the relatively useless Bachelor of Arts in Mathematics. My prior poor school performance didn't prepare me well for the program, so it was a fight all the way through (more persistence!). But, as providence would have it, military science courses were mandatory the first couple years at The Citadel. (The school is a regular liberal arts college with a military-esque atmosphere, but long ago it was the military academy for South Carolina before and during the Civil War.) These classes were run by the various Reserve Officer Training Corps (ROTCs of the Army, Navy, Air Force), and there was no commitment; although, if one became interested, one could take classes beyond the two-year mark and obtain a reserve officer commission at graduation. I chose the naval ROTC class and right away felt a faint calling. In the back of my mind I was well aware that the Navy needed pilots to fly fighter jets that operated off of aircraft carriers—a wondrous thing!

While growing up at the ranch, I had daydreamed about naval aviation, but all along never thought I had what it took to do that glorious vocation. So I kept my desires mostly hidden. To make matters worse, one of the men who was involved in the Atlanta business had been a naval aviator during the '50s, and when I had mentioned my interest in that, he told me that, in his mind, I didn't have what it would take and cautioned me against pursuing it.

In my regular studies I barely got by, but in my naval science courses (ship engineering, weapon systems, navigation, etc.), I really worked hard and excelled. At sophomore year completion they offered to give me a reserve commission upon graduation if I committed then and there, and a bit of money till I finished school—although with no commitment on their part regarding what I might do. Again, feeling the call, I signed and flew back to spend the summer with Mom and Dad.

One day while mending fences on a steep hillside, I told Dad about this commitment. I expected a hearty, "That's great!" but was completely taken aback when he expressed bitter disappointment. I didn't realize that he had assumed that I would return after graduation to assist him at the ranch and in his business enterprises. He would not really fully accept my decision until some years later when he saw firsthand the fruit of my Navy labors.

The last two years at The Citadel were a lot more fun than the first two years, although the non-Navy classes were ever a grind and bore. Heber, my roommate, and I were two peas in a pod, although he was more of a God-fearing and straight-living man than I was then. Nevertheless we got into our share of mischief.

For example, at one point we were disgruntled with the all-quiet policy after midnight. So, along with the help of Art Jordan, one of the nicest guys in H Co., we cut the audio wire about two hundred feet from where it connected to the rooftop Second Battalion megaphone and brought it around the outside of the massive building and into our top floor room through a small hole in the screen. The time was about 3 a.m. The exposed leads were then attached to the back of my two-hundred-watt Sansui amplifier, Boston's debut album was put on the turntable, beginning with "Foreplay-Longtime," and the volume was put halfway up. Cracking the door, we could hear that the music fidelity from the massive megaphone was surprisingly good, so the amp was cranked up to the max without excessive distortion. The concert-level volume immediately jolted everyone out of bed and out onto the balconies with much cursing and gnashing of teeth. Because we had put a large lock of our own on the only roof access, the authorities could not soon gain access to it. Instead, they started going from room to room. We were actually able to play the entire twenty-minute first side and get through some of side two before the authorities got close. As they did, we disconnected the audio wire, and the wire fell out of the window. The Boston LP was then hidden away in the ceiling. The intention was for the wire to fall around the building from our fourth-floor room and come to rest on the "F" Company side so they would get the blame. After some weeks of investigation, the authorities gave up. But there were rumors that probably made it to the Vice Commandant's ear, Colonel Dick. This and other incidences probably had something to do with Heber and I being split up our senior year.

So a *safer* roommate was given me, Mr. Jim Seta by name, who labored hard day and night to achieve a civil engineering degree (much harder than my degree). Jim, who would go on to work for the Army Corps of Engineers and later oversee gigantic private building projects (like whole hospitals), was from Ohio, of Italian stock, and an orderly and disciplined man, yet with a twinkle in his eye. We got on just fine. One night Jim turned a blind eye as I and Art Jordan rammed a foot-long sand pike that Art had caught well down into a classmate's bedframe while he was gone. After a few days the room had to be vacated and fumigators in hazmat suits called in (the classmate forgave us forty years later). On another occasion Jim assisted in depositing much spoiled milk on the room radiator of a battalion staff cadet, whom we thought to be too big for his breeches, while he was out on leave. We then turned the radiator heat full on. Upon his return a week later, fumigators again had to be employed in order to remove the substance that they misidentified as something worse. That one earned us a call from Colonel Dick with threats of expulsion should there be a sequel.

I might mention one more prank. A few days before graduation I asked another fine southern Citadel gentleman in H Co., Mr. Jamie Fiddie (also a fisherman and later a worldwide purveyor of fine aerospace parts), to get me five hundred crickets from his hometown bait shop not far from Charleston. This he did, and a night or two before graduation I was able to get into the military sciences building before sunrise and deposit the crickets in the false ceiling inside. I was a little bit sore at someone in there, but I don't remember who or why. And I don't recall hearing anything one way or the other the next day or later. It may have been a waste of good bait, or maybe there was some salutary effect that was kept strictly confidential. Other stories could be told, but it's time to move on.

As mentioned before, I did very well in the Navy science classes, which were by no means easy. I had nearly all straight *A*'s, but on the final rigorous exam in celestial navigation, when I drew the three position lines on the ocean chart after two hours of intense calculations, the lines did not cross at the same spot. Panic time! So, with only an hour left, I had to start again from scratch. This time with only a minute or two to spare, the lines crossed correctly, which gave me the right position, and I passed. But because I failed on the first try, the instructor, a salty Navy chief petty officer, gave me a *B* for the semester, which disappointed me greatly. The next day I begged him to give me the *A* I deserved, but he wouldn't budge. Maybe I had him on my mind in the cricket affair. Seriously, the chief was very knowledgeable, an effective instructor, and insisted on perfection—because he knew that our lives in the Navy would depend on perfect navigation, something I would soon learn to be true.

Overall, things went quite well for me in the Navy science courses and also on the Midshipman cruise (aboard USS Shreveport) before senior year. Finally the day came when we were told to fill out a "dream sheet." All along the program when asked what I wanted to do, I'd reply, "Oh, Navy logistics or maybe surface warfare." I was embarrassed to say what I really wanted. When that empty form was put in front of me, I clearly remember having the urge, even then, to sell myself short. But I rebuked this familiar spirit and said to myself, *Eric, you'd be a fool not to say what you really want!* So with trembling hand, in the number one slot I wrote *Pilot,* and, wonder of wonders, that's what I got!

My family came to graduation, including Katherine who had the year before graduated from the Naval Academy, my mom's mom (Tennessee Williams saw her that night at a Charleston restaurant and invited her to dine with him!), and even Evelyn, Mom's long-time helper, joined the celebration. The Navy ROTC brass gave my father the privilege of swearing me into the Navy. In a photo from then he is beaming with pride, but he was probably deep down not so sure about my prospects. For now, it was wonderful enough to graduate from The Citadel!

3

Fish Can Fly!

With no break whatsoever in the action, I drove down to NAS (Naval Air Station) Pensacola (Florida) in my brand new '82 Dodge Charger to report for naval aviation orientation training. For two months we learned the basics of Navy military life, aeronautics, and airmanship, and we did much survival training in the pool. That latter training was really tough at times, and dangerous too. In my ten years of naval aviation, the only official test that I ever flunked was the treading water test in full flight gear (that gear included an inflatable floatation vest that was inoperative). Despite growing up around water, the reality was that I was a natural sinker, so all their techniques of *drownproofing* didn't work for me. During that twenty-minute test in water that was over the head, it was an extremely exhausting effort just to keep my mouth barely above the pool surface. I thought I had it made but just before the test ended, one of the instructors said he saw me sink for a moment and push off the bottom. While the rest of the class went on to the next drill, they made me retake the treading water test after a short break. Being already spent, that second try was even more miserable and panic inducing. But I ground my way through and passed. That sure gave me a healthy respect for the ocean should I end up there one day as a result of a mishap.

Speaking of aircraft malfunctions, there were two training devices that simulated, respectively, crashing into the ocean in a fighter jet and a helicopter. With the former, you got in the cockpit (that's all there was, not the whole airplane) and slid down a forty-foot track into the water and flipped over. Then you had to get unstrapped and get to the surface. This "Dilbert Dunker" was more fun than challenging. But the latter device that simulated a large helicopter crashing at sea and sinking down while rolling upside down was nerve-wracking. They had ten or so of us at a time ride the contraption; the problem was that there was only one small exit. Once everyone was strapped in and ready to go, the thing would drop from the ceiling, about twenty feet, hit the water with a jarring shutter, slowly sink another twenty feet, and roll upside down, filling everyone's sinuses with water. Once motion had stopped, everyone had to unstrap and then move along in the line of others till the exit hatch was found. If everyone fought to get out of the hatch first, then no one would get out, so we had to wait in line while our lungs ran out of oxygen. The initial runs went OK enough, but it was difficult to keep one's cool. While there were rescue personnel in scuba gear in the water, it wasn't completely guaranteed that they could get to you in time in case of a problem.

Still, I thought, *This isn't so bad.* Well, until they handed us blindfolds and told us that the final test was to crash and get out of the "Helo Dunker" in complete darkness! "Yes, you have to know how to get out of a crashed helicopter at night too!" they said. With that, a feeling of dread came up. To make matters worse, I was told to sit in the far back of the doomed machine farthest away from the exit port, which was about fifteen feet away with nine fellow aviators (submariners?) in between. As we violently hit the water, took our last breaths, sunk, and rolled over, I kept on telling myself to stay cool and do what we were told. So once motion was stopped, I waited for a bit then slowly started to feel my way along a frame that would eventually lead to a bulkhead and then the escape hatch. Moving too fast only meant getting lots of boot kicks in the face, so I tried to remain calm and go slow. But once I felt the bulkhead and reached over for the exit, all I felt was solid metal. My first inclination was to panic. But I kept my head and retraced my way back along the frame to my original seat and commenced again the route along the frame and bulkhead. By then my lungs were at red alert. This time when I reached out, there was a hole in the fuselage that I was able to squeeze through. A few seconds later I reached the surface and glorious oxygen. If it had taken two seconds longer, I don't think I would have made it.

Then there was live parachute training. To do this, the Navy staff normally put the trainee in a bay near Pensacola, connected him to a parachute that was laid out on the water behind him, then pulled him airborne with a long rope connected to a powerful motorboat. The day I was there, however, the motorboat was broken, so they went to plan "B." Instead of water, they put us on land and pulled us airborne behind a beat-up Navy pickup truck. Our class of about fifty was all there, so this took some time.

All went well—well, till they got to me. They put an old football helmet on my head, strapped a receive-only radio to my chest, and wished me luck. The pickup ahead roared to life on what sounded like six of eight cylinders, the rope tightened, the chute behind me filled, and up I went. The field was not that long, so the tug truck could only get us up to altitude, about three hundred feet, and then stop. Achieving the apex, I immediately started to descend. Looking down, I was reminded of my phobias since youth: heights and deep, dark water. Why did I choose naval aviation?!

Via the radio, they told me to reach up and grab the risers and, once there, pull on the right riser to do a little right turn. This was executed flawlessly, and I was quite proud of myself. Then they told me to pull on my left riser in order to turn left and come back into the wind and prepare to land. I did as instructed, but I and the chute didn't turn. So I pulled harder, but I only continued to veer off course. Then multiple voices came on the radio, so I pulled on the left riser as hard as I could and noticed that not only was I not coming about, but the ground seemed to be coming up awfully fast. The radio's multiple voices turned into multiple yelling voices, but I couldn't understand any of it. With the ground rapidly approaching, I thought it best to assume the knees bent landing position, so I tucked and prepared to roll upon impact. But no tuck and roll occurred when I arrived back on earth but a violent THUD which hurt bad and partially knocked the air out of me.

The staff came running up, yelling, "Don't move!" "Are you OK?!" "Can you feel your toes?" "Who was Abraham Lincoln?" and the like. Turned out that when they radioed to me to grab the risers, my left hand had not only grasped the left riser but had also unbeknownst to me grabbed a lanyard that, when pulled, spilled air out of the chute. As I came down and tried to come back left, all I did was spill air from the parachute, which only made me careen off course and come down faster. Fortunately, I wasn't injured, but I was very sore for some days and, from that time on, leery of parachutes.

During aviation indoctrination, I became friends with my classmate Ensign Mark Sommerfield. He turned me on to a band called Kayak who played wonderful continental progressive rock. One evening, we took a few of his Kayak cassettes and some wine and drove my car up to a park north of town, set my speakers on the roof, and commenced to imbibe and enjoy some epic music. Just when I was at the peak of enjoyment, a policeman drove up and told us to clear out. We complied, but after a little while I made the flawed decision to return. Mark thought this a bad idea, but I insisted. Why should anyone tell us we can't have a good time? So out came the speakers and the wine and, not long after, the same policeman. He had no patience with us this time. So we were arrested and taken in his squad car to the local station. There, we stayed until the Navy shore patrol came and got us.

Now Mark was *really* unhappy with me, and we both thought that maybe our careers were over before they began. All my life it has been as if an angel has been with me and gotten me out of jams, and this time was no different. We both had to go to the county court and were both slapped with misdemeanors of "drunken disorderly" and "disturbing the peace" and were fined. But, to our amazement and great relief, we never heard a peep from the Navy! Mark, who went on to fly Navy patrol aircraft and eventually big jets for FedEx, is to this day still a little sore at me for my stupidity that night. Nevertheless, he remains a good friend and Christian brother.

Once done with the initial aviation indoctrination in Pensacola, we were ready to proceed on to primary flight training. Most students would matriculate at nearby NAS Whiting Field where they would fly the modern Beechcraft T-34 "Turbo Mentor." But there was still one squadron of venerable North American T-28 "Trojan" aircraft still training new pilots down at NAS Corpus Christi, Texas. These lumbering workhorses were older than me at the time and were built around nine-cylinder radial engines left over after WWII (same engine on the Wildcat fighter, Dauntless dive bomber, B-17 "Flying Fortress," etc.). If I were ever to fly anything remotely like those WWII fighters and bombers that I read about as a kid, this would be my only chance! So when they asked for volunteers to go to Corpus, I and one other fellow raised our hands. Turned out that a fair portion of the class was sent there involuntarily. *Needs of the Navy* always came first.

Once in Corpus, Mark and I and three others rented a house. To keep costs down, I set up shop in a part of the garage, putting up plastic tarp walls to keep in the A/C that blew in through the door between the garage and house. When the A/C was on, the walls expanded outward, and the room became pleasantly spacious and cool enough during the hot Texas late summer.

After about a month of ground training in which we learned the mechanical ins and outs of the airplane as well as the procedures to operate it, I had my first flight. US Marine Captain Spencer, a lanky and easygoing Texan, was my instructor pilot. We climbed in the tandem cockpit, he in the back, I in the front, and went through the pre-start checklist. I was right away impressed with the heavy stench of old oil and sweat that emanated from the ancient cockpit that hot summer Texas day. I will also never forget the roar and dense smoke when the engine came to life—an engine that would produce when put to full throttle over 1,400 horsepower! Captain Spencer let me taxi the beast to the runway, but he did the initial takeoff. The roar! The smoke! The glory!

Spencer made the takeoff look easy. Once airborne, he handed the aircraft over to me, and for the first time, I flew—a miracle of miracles and dream come true! He had me turn downwind in the landing pattern in order to prepare for a "touch-and-go" upon the runway from which we just took off. Translated, that simply means to approach the runway, touch down, go full power, and take off again before the end of the runway is reached. So I came in, pulled power, made the final approach, and touched down. I thought, *This is a piece of cake!* Then, per the operations manual, I put the mixture to full rich and moved the prop lever slowly up to 100%. So far so good. Then I brought the throttle up full—and all heck broke loose! Because of the massive engine's torque effect, the plane careened wildly left. In panicked response, I jammed the right rudder, and we veered violently the other way. At that moment two thoughts raced through my head: *This is impossible!* and *We gonna die!*

At that moment, I'll never forget hearing Capt. Spencer hollering in a Texas drawl above the deafening din of the roaring engine: "Yeeeeeeehaaaawww, Yeeeeeeehaaawww!" We continued to crazily careen back and forth, then suddenly the plane became airborne again, and we were safe. I really thought we were finished but didn't realize that Capt. Spencer was *riding* the controls the whole time (he had his own set in the back seat), having seen many previous students blow it the first time they unleashed those 1,400 ponies. It wasn't his first rodeo!

After many more takeoffs and landings, I finally got the hang of it, but the process of wrestling all that power into submission was not easy. Nevertheless, I did quite well overall in the *fam* (familiarization) stage of training. The next flight I vividly recall was my final *fam* check ride with Navy Lieutenant Bolger. If I passed this, I could finally fly on my own—solo! The check ride overall was uneventful. Even the requisite spin test (cross-control the plane until it spins and floats down like a spinning leaf) went according to the book. The only unusual feature was LT Bolger's chain smoking through the flight—something he was known for. This habit intersected with the only mechanical malfunction encountered. On the way back to the field we saw that one of the wing fuel tanks wasn't transferring fuel to the fuselage tank like it should. Through the intercom, LT Bolger said, "No problem, those transfer valves hang up all the time. Just turn the plane over and shake the stick real hard, and the valve will unstick." So I did as instructed: flipped over and shook the craft vigorously. In the blink of an eye, a cloud of butts and ashes filled the cockpit! Bolger yelled for me to straighten 'er back up, but it was too late. Fuel began to transfer normally, but butts and ashes were everywhere. Turns out he forgot to close the covers of his rear seat ashtrays.

The rest of the training went well at Corpus, and I got through the program quickly and with good grades. Flying the Trojan was wonderful once I got used to the powerful torque effect of the big engine. Occasionally an Air Force primary trainer, the jet-powered T-37 "Tweet," would drop into Corpus for refueling, and I'd taxi by that tiny craft in my awesome and smoke-belching Trojan and feel quite superior. The only significant malfunction that I recall was on my first solo flight. All went well, but coming out of a barrel roll the left side engine cowling came unhinged and bulged out from the fuselage about four inches. But that's as bad as it got, and I had no further problems getting back.

As I was finishing my final flights with the *Boomers*, I happened to hear the admin secretary talking to a detailer in Washington, DC. I was quite brash in those days, so I asked the secretary if I could talk to the detailer, which was actually kind of a no-no. She handed the phone to me, and I identified myself and asked the detailer if they could send me next to NAS Meridian, Mississippi, instead of to one of the intermediate jet training bases in barren south Texas. She asked why, and I replied, "Because there are trees in Meridian, and I like trees!" She laughed and said that she would look into it. A few days later I got orders to Meridian.

My time in Mississippi was wonderful, both the six months I was there in intermediate jet training and when, unexpectedly, I returned later for a year-and-a-half instructor tour once I got my wings of gold. NAS Meridian is actually about twenty miles north of the city of Meridian. Much of the base is pine forested, and the land around is rural. Not wanting to live on base, I went around the nearby countryside and knocked on doors and asked if anyone had a room or an apartment or even a house to rent for a short while. The long-time widow Mrs. Mary-Kate Watkins (who had herself worked on the base for many years as a secretary and who turned out to be the spiritual and informational matriarch of the area) connected me with a friend of hers, Mrs. Martha Ellerby, who agreed to rent me her vacant cottage right across the road from Mary-Kate's place. Once moved in, I built a little chicken house and bought five hens, one rooster, and two turkeys. Also, coming out of a nearby country bar one night I heard a "mew, mew" and saw a newborn kitten at my feet in the rainy mud. I raised that kitten, and she became like a best friend dog to me. When I left, I gave the cat to neighbors who had it for another seventeen years. One of the turkeys would beat up on the poor rooster, but one of the hens—a diminutive and super friendly girl—would defend the rooster and beat up on the turkey!

After a day at the squadron—the VT-19 Fighting Frogs—I'd get home and feed my flock, and the phone would ring. It was Mary-Kate. She'd say something like, "Hey, Eric, I have some leftover ham hocks and some fresh green beans from the garden. Would you like some?" So I'd head across the road to her old home and eat like a southern aristocrat. That happened many times. She also invited me to her church, the Lockhart Church of God (Holiness), with Pastor Greer (on his sunset tour of duty) officiating, along with Elder William Hatcher (who was also on the board of nearby Peavey Electronics Corp). I wasn't a believer then, but I'd go occasionally to the church just to be neighborly and out of a vague appreciation for the "ol' time religion." I don't remember much about those services except feeling squeamish when they would drop to their knees between the pews and pray for my salvation. But that squeamishness was more than made up for by their genuine friendliness and down-home southern hospitality.

The training in the North American T-2C Buckeye twin engine training jet all went very well. The only real challenge was that everything now happened at a much faster rate compared to the lumbering Trojan. But unlike that old bird, the T-2 had behind it some relatively modern simulators that helped us get quickly up to speed. Familiarization, night navigation, formation flying, and even a cross-country flight or two went rapidly according to plan, and before I knew it, we began the many FCLP (field carrier landing practice) sessions that led up to our first real aircraft carrier landings. My class of about ten would either fly out or drive to an outlying field way out in the forested country north of the main air station. There, among the countless pines, we would take turns doing many touch-and-goes on the mock carrier flight deck painted on the runway. Half would fly while the other half sat next to the runway in lawn chairs. Then we'd swap out and do it again. Our instructor pilots acted as LSOs (landing signal officers), radioing instructions to us on each pass ("working high," "you're overpowered," "right for lineup," "wave it off!" etc.). One time the wives came along and were amazed at seeing all this action close up.

After hundreds of those practice landings, we were finally ready to go to the ship for the first time—a scary prospect! Naval aviation since its inception had been very unforgiving to both machine and man. The day before we were to do that dangerous thing, we were scheduled to get one more practice session flying out of Pensacola. Some flew there, and I and a few others drove down. On the way I encountered a small turtle (about four inches long) crossing the road. Being a good Samaritan, I rescued the critter and took it with me on down to Pensacola. The next day I wasn't sure what to do with my new friend, so when it was my turn to get my last mock carrier landings, I took him up with me. He turned out to be an excellent co-pilot and rightly earned his wings that day. On the morrow I intended to make him the Navy's first turtle tailhooker, but when I thought about the prospects of the little fellow being slammed around the cockpit upon landing or catapult shot, and maybe becoming entangled in the control wires, I decided to spare us any possible embarrassment. So I returned him back to his natural amphibious environment. It was nice, even for just a short time, however, to have some company in the cockpit.

By the way, I don't recall if we did the day's practice carrier landings at NAS Pensacola or at the nearby NAF (naval auxiliary field) Saufley. If it was the latter, it may be of interest to mention here that this airfield was named after naval aviator #14, LT Richard T. Saufley, who attended the Naval Academy, flew the first naval aviation aircraft in hostile conditions (Veracruz campaign, 1914), and was killed just off Pensacola Bay in the course of attempting to set an airborne endurance record. We are distantly related in that his brother married a lady whose direct ancestor was the first Christian Engleman mentioned at the beginning of this book. Both LT Saufley and Christian Engleman were from what is now Stanford, Kentucky.

The next day we awoke early with great anticipation—and some fear. Few if any budding naval aviators go to the ship the first time fear free, for they know that many an aviator has perished there. And at least a little bit of that fear, or at least healthy respect, remains through his career. Military carrier aviation is a very unforgiving environment, and even for old salts with many tours of carrier aviation duty, certain circumstances (e.g., aircraft malfunction, heavy seas, blacker-than-black night, lack of proficiency, or combo thereof) could always bring back that fear, sometimes to the point of dread and even panic.

But overall I was pretty optimistic that morning. The LSOs were already out on the USS Lexington—the Navy's Pensacola-based training carrier that was kept limping along since WWII—where they were waiting for us. After suiting up and making sure our floatation vests were ship-shape (recall, I was a natural sinker), we climbed into our respective cockpits—alone—and strapped in tight. We were alone because no instructor was crazy enough to ride with a student pilot doing his first carrier operations. One of the fellows I knew in a class ahead of me had trapped (landed) OK but then had something go wrong on the catapult and dribbled off the bow straight down to the water. He ejected just before impact and skipped like a stone on the ocean waves. The ship almost ran him over, but he survived, was fished out of the water, and came back a month later and finished his CQ (carrier qualification) successfully.

So off we went toward the Lexington. They told us to do everything by the book and not look at the ship, other than a glance or two, until we rolled out in the groove on final approach. About one hundred fifty miles out in the Gulf of Mexico, I spotted the ship, but I only glanced. It was just a dot on the hazy horizon. The lead brought us in right over the Lady Lex on the ship's course at three hundred knots and six hundred feet. Then, one by one, we broke into the downwind pattern and dirtied up—i.e., lowered the landing gear—but left the tailhook up because the first two landings were to be touch-and-goes. Abeam the ship about a mile away, but now going the opposite direction, I pulled the power a little, set seven hundred fifty feet per minute rate of descent, and started my turn to final. Crossing over the wake of the ship about three fourths of a mile behind it, I lifted up my eyes for the first time and gasped. I couldn't believe how small it looked! *I can't land on that!* A panic impulse came up, but right away I got it under control with the thought, *Just do it like we trained, and it'll work out.*

So I called the ball, which told the LSOs that I could see the meatball and thus wasn't excessively high or low. The trick was to keep the meatball, a yellow light, between a row of green lights. This carrier landing aid was officially called a Fresnel lens, which was invented by the Brits several decades before. Nearly every landing I had done so far in primary and intermediate training had referenced this Fresnel lens, as they were found not only aboard ship but beside every NAS runway in the world. So I flew the meatball down just as I'd done many times before, kept the plane's angle of attack just right and the plane lined up with the landing area centerline, responded to the LSO calls, slammed down on the deck, threw the throttles to full power, and instantly sprung back up into the air. And I was still alive! The Buckeye, being a light and straight-winged machine, would literally bounce off the deck on a touch-and-go; the A-7 that I flew later would, on a touch-and-go or bolter (hook misses the arresting cables), lumber down the deck while the engine slowly spooled back up and wouldn't start climbing until the ship was in the rear view mirror. The second touch-and-go went well too, with a little less anxiety about the ship size, and then on the third pass—this time with the tailhook down—I trapped aboard the mighty USS Lexington, thus inducting myself into the ancient and honorable order of Navy Tailhookers!

The next step toward my wings of gold was advanced jet training in yet another airplane, the Douglas TA-4J (the training version of the Navy's erstwhile main carrier-based light bomber, the A-4 Skyhawk). I assumed I would carry on with this phase in Meridian, but the need of the Navy was to send me back down to southern Texas yet again—a trip I would make four times before I got to the fleet. So I sadly gave away my cat and chickens (the turkeys had already flown the coop) and bid adieu to Mary-Kate and her blessed friends. I didn't expect to be back, but seems they prayed otherwise.

My Meridian classmates Jeff Walters and Tom Garcia were also shipped out to NAS Kingsville, TX, so we ended up getting an off-base apartment together and began the usual first month at the VT-22 Golden Eagles, grinding through aircraft systems and operations classes. The TA-4J was really a working fleet jet (i.e., a truly manly machine), just with an extra seat for the instructor pilot. There were the typical familiarization, formation, and navigation flights, but now bombing, rocketry, and strafing were added—all using the iron gunsight that naval aviators had used since the beginning. In other words, nothing computerized was employed. It wasn't much different than the gunsight on my .22 rifle. True, you had to factor in a few more things when aiming—if you determined your speed, the angle of dive, and your altitude beforehand (at the point of bomb release or rocket/bullet firing), you could then click the gunsight down so many degrees (or mils) and be set. All you had to do was put the pipper on the target at the right moment and hit the pickle button or pull the trigger. But at that right moment, all the other parameters just mentioned had to be perfect, or nearly so, to hit the target.

At first, bombs and rockets and bullets went flying all over the place. Ground personnel observing the targets would give us instant results: "Eagle 2, your bomb hit was two o'clock at seven hundred feet." But with constant practice there was slow improvement. By my fourth or fifth flight I was getting marksmanship awards left and right and ended the training phase with very good grades.

I mentioned continued formation training in the TA-4J. This was mainly routine and boring. The only exception was the four-plane barrel rolls that we did for the first time in the Skyhawks. Each roll was a case of "crack the whip!" Woe be to the one who was at the end of the whip, and we each got our crack at it. Doing this was both tedious and terrifying and in the process extinguished in me any future desire to be a Blue Angel.

The final phase of training with the Golden Eagles (before final CQ) introduced us to fighter tactics. Here we learned how to dogfight, and it was a hoot. After learning basic fighter maneuvers (unlike the science of bombing, this was more of an art), we went mono v. mono, which I became pretty good at. The last couple flights involved 2 v. 2 battles. I was pretty good at that too, but I found it difficult to keep track of two enemy aircraft while trying to keep track of my wingman. Years later in the fleet, I'd sometimes lose the bubble altogether when participating in mock battles that involved many aircraft on both sides. Providence would soon decide that I was better suited as a bomber pilot than a fighter pilot, although in the end, I'd get that designation too.

In late October 1983, the time came to do a lot of FCLPs and get ready to go to the ship again. It seems the Lady Lex must have had a bilge leak or something, for they told us to fly out west instead and CQ on the USS Kitty Hawk. All went according to schedule, and when we got back, I finished up a few remaining required flights and then in the beginning of December was awarded the coveted naval aviator wings of gold. Because the winging was delayed several times, Dad was not able to attend, but Mom came and proudly pinned on my wings. It was a very special moment. That evening I hosted a party for Mom and my friends where Texas BBQ was served up after roasting over a fire of mesquite wood gathered from the base perimeter. Mom enjoyed meeting my fellow aviators, and they told her humorous stories about me.

Because my grades all the way through were very good, I thought that I'd get fighters for sure. Becoming a fighter pilot was a dream since childhood, despite the fact that I was more of a cutthroat than a rainbow. Two fellows in the class just ahead who did about as well got assigned F-4 Phantoms. Another aviator who I thought maybe did a little better got F-14 Tomcats. I could just feel an "F" coming for me too! The next day the skipper of the Golden Eagles called me in to give me my orders. To my astonishment, I was ordered back to the Fighting Frogs in Meridian—not the kind of "F" I wanted! Turns out my CO there, CDR Frank Wesh, needed instructors and wanted me back. I felt honored by that for sure, and I enjoyed his leadership; in my mind, however, it was a real step back. But you know—the needs of the Navy. So I begrudgingly accepted my fate but not without some grousing to the skipper who gave me the depressing news. Maybe I should have tried to sweet talk the detailer like I'd done in Corpus.

Now there was one good thing about this, and actually more as I would learn later. At this point I could have been, according to the needs of the Navy and the principle of "quality spread," condemned to some antiquated jet-powered transport flying pony express from CONUS to ship ports of call or doomed to some submarine patrol airplane manned by three or four other crewmembers who thought the ultimate thrill was to get a sonobuoy ping off a sperm whale. Speaking of that, another possibility was the antiquated and dilapidated multi-mission plane everyone called "the Whale" that had the Navy designation A3D, which we took to mean "all three dead"—a reference to its crew complement and horrendous accident rate. But with my new assignment of SeRGRAD (selectively retained graduate, sometimes called a plowed back instructor), I would be spared this terrible fate and would instead be guaranteed a tactical fleet seat once my one-and-a-half-year tour of SeRGRAD duty was over. That is, I would for sure get something that flew off the boat and either shot bullets and/or missiles and/or dropped bombs. Every cloud has a silver lining!

I said so long to Jeff and Tom who were also awarded their wings about that time and were both assigned the light attack warfare specialty flying the venerable A-7E Corsair II—Jeff, West Coast; Tom, East. A part of me was happy for them, another part sad that they had to fly that ugly bird that looked like a brick with wings. We'd had a good time living together and had gone on a few fun excursions, one up to San Antonio for a weekend, and another—Jeff and I—to Big Bend National Park where we climbed Emory Peak and overnighted on a ledge of that mountain and watched the evening thunderstorms parade by over the Rio Grande River far below. Five or so years later, all three of us would become Navy adversary pilots.

I also said goodbye to a young lady whom I'd gotten to know in Kingsville. From time to time we would get together and have a fine time. It was a little dicey, though, as she was in the Navy too, enlisted, and worked in the administration section of our squadron. But she promised, and was true to it, that no one would ever find out. In those days there were women in shore-based, non-combat squadrons, and from what I learned over time, there was no way to keep the boys and girls completely apart. This hanky-panky does not help prepare us for life-or-death warfare. Just ask anyone who was at the Battle of the Bulge or the Battle of Midway. That being said, it was a pleasant diversion in the midst of the hectic training pace.

For the fourth and final time, I made the journey between south Texas and Mississippi and returned in not the best of moods to Meridian. The cottage across from Mary-Kate's this time was unavailable, but Elder Hatcher let me rent a small mobile home next to the church. My friends at the Fighting Frogs were glad to have me back, although soon after my return they did something that was quite undignified. While I was out flying one day, learning how to be an instructor pilot, a dozen red roses came to the squadron ready room addressed to "Ensign Engleman." There was a small envelope attached. The bored aviators lounging about decided to steam open the note and take a peek. There, they read, "To Snoogie-oogums from Cuddle-cakes." It was from the gal just mentioned in Kingsville, God bless her, but they didn't know that. When I returned, I was given the roses with much mocking fanfare, and then CDR Wesh stepped forward, shook my hand, and declared, "You are as of this moment no longer 'Blazer' [my self-chosen call sign up till then] but 'Snoogie-oogums'!" As this was decreed, I read the note, realized what had happened, and vehemently protested. As a show of clemency, all agreed with CDR Wesh that the new name should be shortened to just "Snoogie" and that new flight suit name patches be forthwith made to reflect the change. There was nothing I could do, and trying to fight it only made it stick more. So the whole time I was at the Fighting Frogs, and for some time after, I bore this wretched name.

After the initial flurry of re-learning the T-2C Buckeye and how to conduct myself as an instructor pilot, I found the new job to be satisfying and not too stressful, although now there were officer jobs to do. As I recall, they made me assistant administration officer. Through my career I found the flying to be far more in keeping with my temperament than officer duties—the latter consisting partly of political considerations. It didn't take long to realize that I had more time on my hands than during the hectic pace of student days. Noticing the fine forests all around the area, I decided to do something that I'd wanted to do ever since early teen years, but Dad wouldn't allow it: buy an off-road motorcycle, sometimes called a dirt bike.

When about age fourteen, I got my first taste of one and craved one from that time on. My friend Pete Greening and I were going along the power line service road and came upon an injured dirt bike rider, a kid, with his friend. They weren't sure what to do with his broken leg. So Pete and I, being fairly proficient Boy Scouts (his dad, Delbert, was our scoutmaster), got some limbs and string and managed to make a pretty effective leg splint for him. We later heard the doctor was impressed. While Pete was finishing up the job, I asked the kid if I could ride his "motersickle," and he said, "Sure, but watch out—the throttle sometimes sticks wide open!" So I mounted the marvelous machine, thinking, *Just think of where this could take me up in the mountains!,* and got the little Hodaka "Dirt Squirt" engine going and went up a steep trail a ways and turned around. On the way back, indeed the throttle stuck open, and I almost crashed but arrived back intact. From that moment till I bought a Honda XR 200 in Meridian, I never got that kid's dirt bike completely out of my mind. To make matters worse, one of my best friends in high school had a motocross dirt bike, and I would beg him to ride it up and down his driveway.

The four-stroke Honda turned out to be an extremely hard starting bike, so only after a few weeks I bought a two-stroke machine, a Yamaha IT 200, and absolutely loved it. Not long after, I discovered endless forest trails south of Meridian and went there often, sometimes with other squadron fellows who had dirt bikes. An Enduro competition was held there one day, so we decided to field a Navy team in this event that was a combo of racing and keeping as close as you could to a timetable (the goal being to arrive at each checkpoint at a certain time). I rode like mad, with the ribbon time chart streaming behind me, and got fourth place in the 200-cc novice class—a result I was pretty proud of. Because there was no storage shed, I kept the two bikes in the trailer. Thus my living space always had a slight odor of oil and smoke. Because of this, as well as other reasons, Deacon Hatcher could have thrown me out, but he didn't. He was longsuffering, always kind to me, and always praying for me.

One day down at the nearby Lauderdale post office I happened to meet a local lass named Maggie.[1] We got together not long after and became good friends during the time I was based at NAS Meridian. She was a schoolteacher and lived with her parents just down the road. Between her friendship and their hospitality, I was well taken care of. Plus, Mary-Kate and people from the church (which then I only occasionally attended) continued to bless me. When it was all

1. Pseudonym.

over, I probably should have taken Maggie with me and kept her for good. But, to my discredit, I always had too much interest in what was around the next bend of the creek.

All in all, things went pretty well in Meridian. I felt that I was quite good in instructing the new pilots and generally had a good time doing it. But sitting in the back seat with not much to do but observe left me with too much time to think about any discomforts. One that routinely bugged me was scalp itchiness brought on by sweat under the helmet. It would sometimes last the whole flight, and I couldn't wait to get back and itch my head. Also at this time, floaters in my eyeballs' vitreous fluid started to show up, and, having lots of time to notice them, they really became a nuisance. I never said anything to the Navy about this, but on a visit back at the ranch, Dad took me to the Oregon Health Sciences Center for an evaluation. They said there was nothing they could do, as it was a common and insolvable phenomenon. All through my flying career after that I chased little dots in the sky (i.e., the floaters), sometimes mistaking them for other aircraft or even bugs in the cockpit. Today they are even worse, but I do my best to ignore them, which is often not easy to do.

The only close call I had at Meridian happened this way: One day I went up in a two-plane flight, I and my student in the lead aircraft and another instructor and his student in loose formation. Passing through about fifteen-thousand-foot altitude with my wingman about a hundred yards off my right wing and lower, I heard the instructor pilot say over the radio, "Eric, turn left." I told my student who had the stick to gently turn left, which he did. As we got into the turn, again I heard, "Eric, turn left!" but this time more emphatic. So I told my student to turn a little harder, wondering what this was all about. A few seconds later, my wingman yelled urgently, "Eric, TURN LEFT!" So I grabbed the stick from the student and reefed the plane around in a hard left turn, and as I eased the turn I looked back over my right shoulder. To my horror, there was a T-2 with tiger paw tracks over its fuselage—our sister squadron, the Tigers—only fifty or so feet away, climbing by us in a hard left turn. In an instant the interloper passed by and then went out of sight above us, but I was very shaken. My student never saw the Tiger T-2, which was just as well as he might have soiled his flight suit. We continued on with the mission, but I was very anxious to get back and find out how this could have happened.

Safely back aboard NAS Meridian, my wingman (the instructor) told me that as we climbed out he noticed another T-2 far below us climbing even faster. Because it looked to him like the mystery T-2 might get close to us as he climbed, my wingman told me to turn left so as to get out of his way. But as I did, the interloper turned left too. So he told me to turn harder left, but the T-2 came harder left too. Seeing that the intruder was about to hit me as he climbed through our altitude, that's when my wingman yelled at me to turn left. Without that last "Eric, TURN LEFT!" I and the Tiger T-2 would have coalesced into a big fireball. Even still, it was a very close call. But, as I found out when I then walked over to the Tiger's ready room, my wingman's calls were just what got me into the jam in the first place.

I figured out which Tiger instructor pilot had just returned from flying, found him, and said, "Do you know that you came this close to colliding with me today?" Looking surprised, he replied, "No, Snoogie, I don't know what you're talking about. I didn't see a thing. But I did wonder why someone kept on telling me to turn left." When he said that, it dawned on me what had happened. This Tiger pilot's first name was, like mine, Eric, and because my wingman had used my common first name in his urgent calls instead of my dreadful and uncommon call sign "Snoogie," it created confusion that almost killed four of us that day. Holy jumpin' Jehoshaphat! Not long after, I got a *Naval Aviation Safety Journal* (aka *Approach*) article published called "A Tale of Two Erics" that retold this incident and made the case that it is safest to use unique call signs or identifiers in flight.

Near the end of my one-and-a-half-year SeRGRAD commitment, the skipper called me in and told me what my next orders would be. I was still hopeful for fighters but was ready to accept something less. Since I had come back to the Fighting Frogs, any future assignment would not be primarily based upon my piloting skills as it was when I was a student pilot but upon how good an officer I was. In that realm, I knew I was so-so at best. So when the skipper told me I got West Coast Light Attack (i.e., A-7s based at Lemoore, CA), I was somewhat disappointed but not surprised. Little did I know then what a blast it would be, and that through this God would draw me to Himself.

Before checking out from VT-19, I was sent out with a group of students who were to CQ for the first time. My job was to get some traps too, if the opportunity arose, and in general help look after the "chicks." The Lexington again was apparently unavailable, so they sent us to the West Coast and the USS Enterprise. Even today when the subject of the Enterprise comes up (the ship is now out of the fleet), I tell people that, on June 19th, 1985, I got one trap on the "Big E" only because the ship's "air boss" (and maybe the captain) was smokin' mad at me. Here's the story.

We flew out to the Enterprise from, as I recall, NAS North Island—San Diego. The weather was good, and things went quite well as the Frog students got their first carrier landings on that famous ship. Being low priority, I just circled overhead and waited. After a while, the air boss, who controls all airborne traffic near the ship, finally cleared me in for a couple of touch-and-goes. The first one went fine, but on the second approach close in the air boss told me to "wave off" and to "steer pigeons home plate," which meant "go home." So, a little miffed that I didn't get more action, I went full power and cleaned up, but instead of immediately climbing, I "hot dogged" it just a bit and flew by the ship's island (in which sits the air boss and captain) pretty close by and fast. Once past the ship, I started climbing and pointed in the direction of San Diego. About halfway back to shore, I received a radio transmission from the Enterprise with an order to return to the ship, trap, and see the air boss. I immediately perceived that they had taken umbrage at my pass by the island. So I turned around and started to worry about what awaited me there.

Approach and trap aboard the Big E went OK, and after getting chained and shut down, I was told to go to Flight Deck (the room where flight deck aircraft movements are coordinated) and wait. After some time, the air boss abruptly entered wearing a yellow shirt with a stenciled "AIR BOSS," with carotid and temple arteries bulging. He got in my face and severely chewed me out for a good couple minutes—words to the effect of, "you're a jerk," "who do you think you are?" "you imperiled the whole ship," "throw your wings overboard," and "your career is finished." He finally gave me a chance to respond, so I nervously recounted to him how I was waved off close in and had some fun going by the ship but honestly didn't think it was a big deal—which was true. He started in again berating me, but to my relief I noticed the condemnation had become a bit less severe as he went on, such that when he was done with me, the threat level had gone from "you're finished!" to "you're finished if you ever do that again!" Then he commanded me to get the heck off his ship with orders never to see his face again. I replied, "Yes sir," did an about face, got back in my waiting jet, fired up, catapulted off, and headed back to home plate with my tail between my legs. I was pretty shaken, but on the other hand, I was pleased that I had logged a landing on, and catapult off, the mighty USS Enterprise—even if it had not been under the best of circumstances.

When finally back at Meridian, I braced for some post-incident impact, but it never came—to my great relief. Maybe the Big E's air boss forgave me after all. Some days later, my SeRGRAD duty done, I said goodbye to my Fighting Frog friends, bade farewell to Mary-Kate and the church friends, struggled through a tearful goodbye to Maggie, and headed west to do my tour of duty at the tip of the American sword.

4

Learning to Operate a Fearsome Weapon

The drive from the pine forests of Mississippi to the creosote-bush-bedecked Mojave Desert of south California was uneventful, except for a tire that developed a softball-sized boil passing through broiling Needles, CA. For the moment I was driving a well-used BMW that I bought from a Meridian squadron mate after my Charger spontaneously combusted one night. Upon arrival in Lemoore, which was in the middle of the San Juaquin Valley (the "breadbasket of the world"), I was surprised how hot and dry and dusty it was. NAS Lemoore was surrounded mostly by cotton- and vegetable-producing fields as far as the eye could see, and the evidence of farming was everywhere: migrant workers, fresh vegetable stands, tractors, plows, harvesters, trucks hauling produce, and routine appearances of crop dusters. Speaking of the latter, in a few months they would spray the cotton with defoliant (maybe a derivative of *Agent Orange*?) and the odor of that, along with the dust and pesticides and smog already there, would produce a plethora of respiratory and lung ailments.

At first I stayed in the BOQ, but after meeting several classmates at our introductory class at the VA-122 Flying Eagles, four of us ended up renting a house together. For the six months that it took to learn the A-7E, we were always together either at work or at home. What a good time it was! I, Larry Baldauf, Paul Barney, and Greg Landis were four peas in a pod. When we went to our fleet squadrons, we didn't see each other as much, as one or more were at sea. But when we did, it was usually a party.

The curriculum in learning to fly the A-7 was somewhat the pace and form as previous squadrons in the training command but with even more bombing and strafing—and something else that I thoroughly loved: low level flying. In fact, that was the bread and butter of the A-7 mission: come in low and fast so as to remain undetected and put bombs on target. Now it is one thing to fly low and fast over flat boring territory, like I had done a few times over Texas and Mississippi. But on my first flight flying out of Lemoore, I found out that our local military operating area (MOA) was not over Lemoore but over the magnificent mountains and valleys east of there, stretching from the Sierra Nevada mountain range, across the Owens Valley, up over the Inyo range, down across Saline Valley, and on into what is known today as Death Valley. Between mountain tops and valley bottoms, there was sometimes ten thousand feet of change, and it was all so gloriously beautiful. I couldn't believe my good fortune! To fly at 500 mph averaging about two hundred feet above the ground over that kind of terrain was stupendously wonderful! Any disappointment about not getting fighters evaporated when I found out that the A-7 was a fine machine and that its mission was a blast—especially as practiced in California, and later, Nevada.

On one of my long-distance, low-level training flights, in a two-seat TA-7C with Rhino in the back seat, we flew high level out to central Utah, then turned around and flew low level to the NAS Fallon NV bombing range, then high level back to Lemoore. That was another good thing about the A-7: you could fly a long way. Coming back west, hugging the dirt at 420 nautical miles per hour (*knots*, which are a little longer than statute miles), we roared right over the top of Wheeler Peak—now a National Park—in far eastern Nevada, just skimming the glaciers there. After another craggy ridge or two, we settled down in a long sagebrush-covered valley. Rhino said over the intercom, "Snoogie, if you get into combat, you might have to go extremely low—so let's practice that here. Just slowly step it down so you can see what it's like."

I didn't realize it then, but Rhino, while being a smiling and good-natured fellow, was a deadly serious professional when it came to the mission. This exercise, which honestly scared me some, was not for fun but for contingent combat survivability. So, from the approved above-the-ground distance of two hundred feet, I nudged the nose over a bit, thinking that he would be proud of me if we made it down to one hundred. Once there, the sagebrush was whizzing by even faster.

"How's that?" I said.

"That's good. Now let's step it down to fifty."

With this, I felt a slight pucker in my backside, but I complied, pushed the stick forward again ever so gingerly, and saw the radar altimeter go from one hundred to seventy to fifty. The sage bushes were now just streaks, and I wondered if Rhino knew of every possible power pole or laundry line out there. He didn't say anything, so we stayed there for what seemed like a long time. I could see the next mountain range starting to loom in the distance, so I suggested we go back up. I'd seen enough. But Rhino said, "No, let's come down a little more."

I gulped, tried to reign in my nerves, and nudged the stick over with nothing but a thought and saw the radar altimeter go forty-five . . . forty . . . thirty-five . . . thirty. If I had flinched or flatulated at that point we would have been done. That's the lowest number I saw. All at nearly 500 car miles per hour! Rhino quietly said, "That's enough."

All was a blur going by—well, all except for what I saw on the starboard (right) side just at that moment, a snapshot that is forever etched in my memory: There, about a hundred feet away, were several scrawny black cows, and amongst them was a scrawny cowboy on a scrawny horse looking right at us wildly waving his cowboy hat over his head. I'm sure he was yelling, like Capt. Spencer two years before, "Yeeeehawwww, yeeeehawwww!" Or maybe he was just cursing us. I just hope that he still had his hearing when he went to bed that night.

We made it back home OK. That exercise was nerve-wracking but valuable. During the next six years, I operated Navy bomber and fighter aircraft often very close to the ground in all kinds of scenarios.

This prepared me for that. Had I ever been in combat, the lesson would have been even more valuable because wartime airborne operations had shown again and again that *sometimes* staying as close to the deck as possible was the only way to accomplish the mission and survive. Later I would come to respect Rhino even more as a professional and humane person. He would also on a couple occasions call me out when I was something less than professional.

You might be wondering about the A-7E Corsair II. What shall I say? If I'd flown the F-14 Tomcat, I would say that she was supersonic and sexy as a Lamborghini. But I flew the A-7, so I'll say it was subsonic and sexy as a UPS truck. It didn't turn any heads—well, not unless it was roaring by you a hundred feet away at 500 mph! The Navy fighter jets were based at NAS Miramar in San Diego. Droves of single ladies in mini skits and high heels flocked there in response to seeing the sleek Tomcats flying over affluent San Diego County. Meanwhile, the sight of a Corsair lumbering overhead the farms of Tulare County prompted the dairy daughters there to glance up for a moment, then turn back, unimpressed, to their milking. A few, however, would think about their situation and contemplate that maybe one of the men in those ugly jets might be the ticket out of the San Juaquin Valley dustbowl. So, we had a few regular ladies show up at the Lemoore Officers' Club (O'Club), and although of the farm girl sort, I was happy to have them. They were always cheerful and up for a good time.

Back to the A-7. During the sixties, the A-4 Skyhawk had been the main carrier-based light bomber and had served well. Thousands of them were thrown into the Vietnam conflict and hundreds were shot down. The Navy figured it needed something that could survive better, carry more bombs, and get those bombs on target better using updated aiming technology. Several companies offered designs, but the Navy chose Vought Aeronautics' offering, which was loosely based on the legendary Vought F-8 Crusader fighter (my dream of dream fighters—sadly retired by my time).

The "A" version was quite a dog, and the targeting system wasn't very good. The "E" version that I flew was much better. It had pretty good power (although no afterburner) and a computer-run targeting system that considered all kinds of factors and put targeting symbology up on a head's up display (HUD) in front of the pilot. If this targeting system crapped out, you could still do the age-old way of targeting, as I had done in the TA-4J in Kingsville, although only through the HUD. If that display failed, you could still bomb but only by eyeballing your release. Later I did that from the back of an F-18 Hornet and did amazingly well.

Gone was the need, like in the Skyhawk, to preplan your release at a certain dive angle, speed, elevation above the ground, and setting on the iron gunsight. In the A-7E you could come to the target about any way you wanted, designate the target once in sight by moving a little dot on the HUD with a little joystick by the throttle and pressing a button on top of the joystick, then fly the airplane up a line on the HUD while depressing the "pickle" button on the control stick. When the computer figured out that you were at the right release point that would get the bomb to the target, it would release the bomb automatically. This was late sixties and early seventies technology, but boy, it was deadly accurate!

Another targeting option that was in my mind, not quite as accurate but easier to use, was put a little cross up on the HUD. As long as you were in a steady dive, that cross would tell you where the bomb would hit if you hit the pickle right at that instant. Thus all the pilot had to do was fly the cross up to the target and hit the pickle button. The Corsair's computer did the rest. The computer and HUD also provided targeting for rockets and strafing with the A-7's Mark 61 Gatling gun—a device that put out four thousand bullets per minute (and that's on the "low" setting!).

The A-7 did more than that. The tactical manual that gave us instructions on how to use any of the weapons that the Corsair carried looked like a gigantic family Bible. A few of the other weapons we dabbled with were "Shrike" and "HARM" anti-radiation missiles (that would target enemy surface-to-air missile sites), anti-ship mines, and a gigantic TV-guided glide bomb called the Walleye. There were other weapons as well, and it was hard to keep proficient with them all.

Underway on "cruise" we usually carried a Sidewinder air-to-air missile that could be employed to shoot down enemy aircraft. We could also use the Gatling gun (the Tomcat had the same gun) for that purpose if necessary. Speaking of air-to-air, we did train some in fighter combat, but the A-7 couldn't keep up with modern fighters in a dogfight. To make matters worse, the automatic maneuvering flaps/slats that would have given us a fighting chance were, during my tour of duty, off limits due to cracks. At sea we would off and on be the resident bogies for the fighters, so air-to-air combat skills could be developed. Because energy was precious in a dog fight (altitude and speed and power), you had to learn to fight the Corsair with an extremely gentle touch so that energy would be preserved. That gentle touch would really help me when I would serve later as a naval adversary pilot.

To summarize, the A-7 was a multi-mission machine that could do wondrous things but was difficult to fly around the ship, and the exotic suite of weapons and navigation systems tended to overload the pilot. There was simply too much to do. Not a few Corsair pilots disappeared at sea over the years no doubt, at least for some because they had become overloaded and lost control of the situation. Later, fighter-bombers would go to two-man cockpits to take burdens off the pilot, and accident rates went down as a result. In general, I much preferred single seat flying, but the tendency to get overloaded almost bit me hard on a few occasions. Plus, there were relatively few officers in the squadron to do the many officerial jobs. Thus, whether in the air or aboard ship, there was too much to do.

The process of learning to fly the A-7 with the Flying Eagles went very smoothly—except at the CQ phase at the very end. Just before we began training to go to the ship, our class went down to NAF (Naval Air Facility) El Centro, near the Mexican border just east of San Diego, for about a week to fine-tune our bombing and strafing skills. I drove down with my dirt bikes in tow, and others either flew or drove. On a couple occasions after the morning flight, Bob Playfair (a capable outdoorsman and good friend by that time) and I would ride the bikes from nearby Plaster City out onto the target area near the bombing and strafing bullseyes. After a little while, our buddies would show up to attack the target, and we'd enjoy the spectacle up close. None of the bombs used at El Centro were live. Only a puff of smoke would result when they hit the ground, so there was not much danger. On the other hand, we had to be a little more careful when they came in to strafe. Perhaps the greatest danger occurred when the "Duck" spotted us. The Duck was a two-engine Cessna prop job manned by a couple of our instructors with the mission of yelling for us to pull out of a dive if any of us got target fixation (a strange and unpredictable phenomenon that had killed dive bomber aviators before). The Duck pilots knew we were out there, and, once spotted, they buzzed us and nearly gave us a haircut. A day or two later I rode in the back of the Duck and was quite nervous as we weaved our way between the sand dunes on the way to the target. During my time with the Flying Eagles I was amazed that they never cracked-up a Duck—a testimony to the aviating excellence of the instructors.

It was during this time at El Centro that I was finally freed from the wretched "Snoogie" call sign. All these years I had a specific memory of how that happened. My good friend, CDR Len "Peewee" Fox, who was on that same El Centro detachment, however, told me a different story as we recently backpacked and fished the Wind River range of Wyoming. I much prefer his version, especially in view that he was not drinking at the time (he never has) and would therefore have better recollection than I. But I'll briefly tell my version and then his and let the reader decide.

One evening we—students and instructors—walked out of the Officers' Club after having a few, perhaps more than a few, drinks. I then climbed up in a tree and, from near the top, started spouting off guru-like wisdom. "Rhino," an instructor whose call sign was based on his skin texture, looked up and declared, "From now on, you will be known as 'The Bhagwan'!"—"The Bhagwan Shree Rajneesh" being the self-deifying and free-love guru of an anything-goes commune in Oregon who was then in the process of being deported. Peewee's version goes like this: When we were still in the O'Club, the instructors, including Rhino, had decided to call me "The Bhagwan" because my bombing and strafing scores were so good, it was as if I was—like the Bhagwan—tied into the cosmic harmonic convergence of the universe. "That's why they decided to call you 'The Bhagwan,'" concluded Peewee. So now, dear reader, you can decide which story is best.

At all events, I was glad to be rid of "Snoogie," but being from the area where the Bhagwan Shree Rajneesh had his commune, and thus knowing a little bit about him, I wasn't entirely enthused about the new name. The man was a nut job, and when he died a few years later in India, a neighbor gave this epitaph: "Thank God he's dead—he was a nuisance." But it's the name I bore for the remainder of my Navy career. Maybe "Snoogie" was better after all.

By and by we finished the bombing detachment and returned to Lemoore. Then, in short order we returned to El Centro for lots of FCLP (field carrier landing practice) in preparation for yet another CQ—this time on the USS Ranger. The practice landings in El Centro went fine, but I had some misgivings because the Ranger CQ would involve night work for the first time. My misgivings were based somewhat upon what I had recently experienced in the Night Carrier Landing Trainer back in Lemoore. Allow me to briefly describe what I learned to call "the torture chamber."

When I first went in the Night Carrier Landing Trainer device, I thought it wouldn't be that hard. I was wrong. This crude simulator was old technology by then and only had a small TV-like screen just ahead of the HUD in the cockpit. I still recall my first time in it. Once inside, I expected to go through the engine start routine, then be put on the downwind by the instructor (who sat just outside at a console) in order to allow for a long straight-in to the ship. But no sooner had I strapped in, the instructor said over the intercom, "I'm going to put you three miles behind the ship. Good luck!" And shazam! I was suddenly there and flying.

Right away I was struck by how dark it was. Other than the faint red dot that was the ship, it was an abyss of black three-dimensional space. There were zero visual clues from the outside how to fly the machine, so I immediately went to the instruments and went straight ahead until I intercepted a three-degree glideslope and started down. As I tried to keep a steady 750 fpm (feet per minute) rate of descent and transitioned to flying the meatball, some vertigo started creeping in, the engine response seemed terribly slow, every correction turned out to be a gross overcorrection, and it was as if I was drunk. At about a mile, the meatball went low, so I added power, and nothing happened. The instructor, acting as LSO, said, "Power!" So I added a little more, and the meatball went flying up to the top of the lens. Then I heard, "Easy with it, you're high." So I pulled a little power and nudged the nose over, and suddenly the meatball fell and turned red, meaning I was really low approaching the back of the ship. The instructor said emphatically, "Power! POWER!" and then "WAVE OFF! WAVE OFF! WAVE OFF!" But it was too late. The moment I hit the simulated stern of the ship and exploded in a fireball, the TV screen froze, and the instructor said, "Not bad. Let's try it again."

And so we did, but I was already shaking and sweating. I distinctly remember thinking, *It can't really be this bad!* But as I would soon learn, it was. No matter how much of a hot shot a pilot was, this device would lay him low. It was deadly realistic. I loathed this machine, but it prepared me well for what was to come in that I did not thereafter take night carrier landings for granted. Over many sessions I got a little better at it but not much—so I faced the real deal with some trepidation.

After many FCLP sessions at El Centro we got ready to go to the Ranger, which was somewhere off the coast of California. Our instructors, who would be our LSOs, told us that we'd get most or all of our day's work done the next day, even a night landing or two if possible. We needed something like ten day traps and six night traps to qualify, which might take two or three days to complete. My hope was to do well enough to qualify for a USS Midway endorsement. You had to be above average to go to the air wing on that ship because she was forward deployed in Japan and so was always in a state of readiness. This, as we'll see, was not to be for the adventurous me.

The next morning after some fitful sleep, I turned on the TV just as I was leaving the BOQ room, and there, in real time, I saw the space shuttle gloriously go up—and blow up. That was the end of the Challenger. That got me off to a bad emotional start. We took off and flew west, passed over San Diego, and within an hour found the Ranger which was steaming along on smooth seas. The weather was good, and so the day traps and cat shots went fine. After the sun went down, they sent me back out. According to my logbook, I flew an hour that night and logged one touch-and-go, one bolter (touched down but missed the wires), and four traps. I don't recall it being a traumatic experience. Turned out to be beginner's luck.

The next day I went airborne for an hour and quickly banged out six day traps. They needed to get other fellows up that night, so

I didn't fly. On the third day out, January 31, 1986, I still needed a couple of day traps and three night traps to qualify. When a plane came available, the day traps were quickly bagged; then I waited for night. In view of how things went the first night, I was confident that the last three night traps could be obtained with relative ease. But circumstances change.

Late in the afternoon the ship started moving around, and by sunset the ship was heaving so much that the order came down for everyone to stay below decks unless there was an absolute need otherwise. I wondered if flight ops would be scrubbed, but to my surprise the show went on for us and the S-3 Viking (anti-sub twin jet) training squadron that was also aboard. So once it got dark, out we went. Trying to inspect the parts of the plane hanging out over the rough ocean was unnerving in the faint orange glow of the deck lights and with the deck rolling this way and that. Taxiing to the cat was challenging too because one moment you're taxiing uphill and a few seconds later sliding downhill as the ship rolls. Some clouds had rolled in too, so the night was really dark, and there was no moon. Going off the catapult into the utter black void knowing you're only sixty feet off the water is also a trip. In an instant you go from visual cues to absolutely none, so there is no other option than to immediately go to your instruments and start a rate of climb.

The next three hours that night would turn out to be a nightmare. From the initial cat shot to the final trap, I had an almost incapacitating feeling of dread. It was entirely all I could do to keep it together. It took me *nine* tries to get aboard *three* times. The whole while, our LSOs and the S-3 LSOs were yelling and sometimes screaming at those making their final approaches, which unnerved us even more. I got the urgent "WAVE IT OFF!" six times that night because I was so far out of whack. The night landing simulator in Lemoore—that torture chamber—turned out to be right after all! But it was now worse because of the high seas and especially because this was no simulation. To this day I recall the thought that I would have when I would finally get aboard: *What?! They're sending me up to the cat again? This is insane! Can't they see that I'm a wreck?!* But the part of me that didn't want to fail kept driving me on. I wanted them to end the madness, but I wasn't willing to end it myself, which I could have. Speaking of that, even though not that far away from the coast and several military bases with nice long *unmoving* runways, that option never crossed my mind. For me, I may as well have been a thousand miles from anywhere in the middle of the Indian Ocean.

After getting my last required trap, the "deck apes" taxied me over to deck's edge, chained the jet down, and motioned for me to shut off the engine. I was utterly physically and emotionally exhausted. With knees weak and the ship heaving, it was a job just to make it back to the ready room. A little bit later they shut down flight operation altogether seeing that few were getting aboard and with the thought that someone was probably going to get killed if they continued. Then the LSOs came around to debrief us. They said that I had not responded promptly to their calls, and while they would pass me, they could not give me the Midway endorsement. I was incredulous. How could they send us into the lion's den and fault us for coming back with wounds? They should have praised us for surviving the ordeal! Man, that burned me up. Out of our A-7 group of eight, only I and one other passed. The others had to come back a month or two later. Between us and the S-3 bubbas, I heard that the boarding rate was only thirty percent that night. That is, only one out of every three or four attempted landings actually got aboard. We were very fortunate that no one was lost.

Now looking on the bright side, as it would turn out, I would continue to have problems at night (as we shall see) once I was out in the fleet. So the decision that night not to send me to the Midway perhaps saved my life. (An A-7 pilot had not long before perished on the stern of the Midway.) Also, as soon as I went to the ship that I would serve on eventually, the USS Carl Vinson, I met a fellow aviator who would over the next four years lead me to Christ. Thank You, God, for unexpected heavy seas, and thank you, LSOs, for keeping me off the round down that night and for not letting me go to the Midway!

You might wonder what caused the heavy seas that night. I recall that when we got back to El Centro, we read a newspaper that told of the San Diego area beaches being torn up by big waves caused by an earthquake off the coast of Hawaii. We did our CQ in a tsunami! Recently, I wondered if my recollection (thirty-seven years later) was correct regarding that. I was sure about the big waves, but the tsunami part seemed far-fetched. So, before starting this book, I did a little research. I found nothing about an earthquake/tsunami from online archived newspaper sites nor government sites (e.g., USGS, NOAA), but I did find an article from a Santa Cruz paper all about how—on the same day/night of this event—the beaches and pier were destroyed by giant waves from a powerful storm just off the coast. So that's what it was, and at the time we knew nothing about it. Apparently we were just south of the storm but were affected by swells that emanated from it. I don't know how I got the tsunami thing in my head. Who knows? Maybe there was a tsunami, and I just didn't find the record of it. Romans 8:28 says that "God causes all things to work together for good to those who love God." I didn't love the Lord then, but I knew about Him. Nevertheless, He worked that dreadful experience for my good. I just didn't know it at the time.

5

The Tip of the Sword
and
the Mercy of God

After returning to Lemoore I was assigned to the VA-27 Royal Maces—aka the Chargers—attached to Carrier Air Wing 15 aboard (when at sea) the USS Carl Vinson. Our squadron CO was then CDR Joe "Mafia" Sciabarra, and CDR Malcolm "Mal" Branch was the XO (executive officer). The Vinson was nuclear powered and then the newest carrier in the fleet. They were just starting workups getting ready to go on cruise later that year. Turned out I needed the practice. We would go out to sea for three or four weeks just off the coast, get lots of experience operating around the ship, and return again to Lemoore where the operational tempo would continue just over land. On the Vinson I was assigned a stateroom with two other comrades: my fellow aviator Michael "Pasta" DellaPolla and a new ensign to help with the administration of the squadron, Chuck Meek. We fit in well together, but the quarters were less than optimal.

We were directly under catapult #2. When a Tomcat came to the cat, only a few feet above our bunks, and went full afterburner, it was like he was in bed with you. The noise was horrendous. Plus, the piping for the high-pressure water that kept the JBD (jet blast deflector) from burning up passed through the room and roared like crazy when in use. And as a bonus feature for us low-ranking pollywogs, the retrieving cable that went and brought back the steam-powered catapult piston (about the size of a telephone pole) after each cat shot also passed around a couple of sheaves in our room, emitting a deafening whine as the mechanism went back and forth after each shot. Napping during flight ops was hopeless, and even when things quieted down for the night, the noise transmitted through the deck from tugs and huffers and dragging chains and dropped chocks, etc., prompted us to wear earplugs. Nevertheless, I was content as a clam.

Perhaps my best friend in the squadron ended up being our ordnance officer, CWO (chief warrant officer) Patrick Walters. He knew when to have a good time, knew when to be serious, and was willing to explore the mountains with me on dirt bikes. When ashore, he and his wife, Linda, showed me wonderful hospitality, and when we went to sea, he kept my Corsair amply supplied with the finest of munitions.

Not all that we had to know was learned beforehand. Even though I was now in a fleet squadron, there was still much OJT (on-the-job training) to do that made me wiser and more knowledgeable. For example, just after one of my first cat shots off the Vinson, an A-6 Intruder tanker (who had been shot off just after me) came up close by with his hose out and the pilot looking at me. I had no idea what he wanted. Then the pilot gave me the well-known "get your head out of your you-know-what" signal. After a few more perplexing seconds, it dawned on me that he probably wanted me to check if his buddy store would pass gas or not. So, assuming this was the case, I extended my probe, went behind him (still skimming the water getting away from the ship), and plugged in. A few seconds later, apparently content that fuel had transferred, he retracted the hose and went his way. It was something like inspiration that helped me put two and two together, for before that time, I didn't know that tanker pilots, right after launch, desire a check of their fuel transfer system to know if the system is "sweet" or not.

It was about this time that I had a really bad night at sea. One thing to keep in mind is that a pilot having trouble getting aboard holds up the whole show—for both other aircraft in the air and for the mother ship. Especially when on cruise, the ship is usually on a tight timetable and must spend most of its time proceeding to the next destination. An aviator who struggles to get aboard interferes with this because he forces the ship to steam into the prevailing wind until he is safely back on deck. This does not make the battle group admiral nor the captain of the ship very happy.

I don't recall too much about that night other than there was a low cloud deck that made things blacker than black below it and that with each yelling "WAVE IT OFF!" I became increasingly unhinged. It's hard describing the feeling of being strapped tightly inside a roaring fifteen-ton machine in three-dimensional utter blackness over an unseen black ocean abyss, trying to put the ill-handling machine on a little dot of faint orange light out there in space knowing your life depends on it. Other nights I had held it together, but not this one. After the fourth or fifth attempt, with that sense of dread come upon me like it had at the Ranger, I climbed above the cloud deck on the downwind, looked up and saw stars, and said sincerely, "God, help me!" Not a second later, the sound of a chicken cackling came over the radio, and without hesitation I believed that the Creator of the universe, and sustainer of it too, was trying to loosen me up with the same sound that had comforted me as a boy.

A few minutes later I turned to the ship's final course, followed the instruments down through the clouds, and sighted the ship and the meatball. Then, just before calling the ball, I heard the chicken again, which made me smile, and thirty seconds later I was home and dry. Every carrier-based naval aviator can tell you about the violence of a trap yet in the same breath tell you what a relief it is to know that you're safely aboard. Being slammed forward in the straps that night never felt so good.

But the LSOs representing the ship's skipper and others weren't so happy, and they warned me sternly that if I didn't get my act together, they'd have to ground me until they could figure out what to do. "You can't be holding up the show!" In reply, I admitted that I was struggling but asked them to be patient and keep sending me out at night so I could maybe conquer my fears. Then I asked, "Which one of you gave the chicken calls?" They didn't reply but looked at each other then at me in a way that showed that I'd better drop the matter. So I left it at that. Thankfully they were longsuffering in regard to me, and I did begin to improve my night landing performance, but it wasn't easy. One little thing that helped was my harmonica. From that time on, I always carried my harmonica at night. I'd try to arrive in the stack a little early where I was low enough to remove my oxygen mask for a minute and play a couple bars of "Oh Suzanna" or "Camptown Races" or even "Margaritaville." This helped in calming the jitters.

I'm always tempted to leave the chicken story there in order to get maximum spiritual bang for the buck. But in the name of transparency, let me tell you the rest of the story. A week or two later, I was recounting the incident to a friend in the pilot's "dirty shirt" wardroom when one of the fighter crew members sitting at the table suddenly looked my way and said, "Oh yeah, that was me," and went on to say something about it being some secret communication between he and another airman in the air wing. Well, maybe that was him. But in nearly twenty years of aviation, that was the first time and the last time that I ever heard chickens on the radio. Even if that was him, just like God made a donkey speak perfectly timed words to the duplicitous prophet Balaam when he was hired by the king of Moab to curse Israel (Numbers 22), He could have very well prompted that fighter RIO (radar intercept officer) to squawk like a mother hen that just laid an egg—"for nothing is impossible with God." In any case, I was just happy to be aboard and alive, and I sensed then that God had something to do with it. That RIO didn't know that I needed those two chicken cackles (if he gave them), but God did!

For the next few months we alternated between land and sea until ready to be placed on the tip of the American foreign policy spear. In August of 1986 my naval squadron VA-27 (*V* from Latin *Volare*, "to fly," *A* meaning "attack"—i.e., bomber) joined CAG 15 (Carrier Air Group) based onboard CVN 70 (the Vinson, *C* meaning "carrier," *V* meaning "she carries mainly *V* squadrons"—i.e., fixed-wing aircraft, *N* meaning "nuclear powered") for a six-month Pacific and Indian Oceans cruise. The ship initially steamed north-northwest instead of the usual west. The plan was to show the Soviets for the first time since WWII that we could operate effectively near their desolate Siberian eastern coast. So we cruised up through the Gulf of Alaska and then passed westward along the Aleutian Islands on the Bering Seaside. Flying along that island chain was eerie, with smoking volcanoes and enormous glaciers here and there, and the ocean everywhere in a state of foamy turbulence. Three of my four transits across the Pacific on the Vinson would be along the far north route of the Aleutians. One of the pleasant memories is of the "Puffin" sea birds with their big multi-colored beaks, flying in formation with me only a few feet away while I'd be inspecting an airplane before a flight. They'd look me right in the eye, and I'd wonder what was going through their minds. They might have wondered the same. This first passage up north was not so bad, but the return passage five months later in the winter would prove much more challenging.

Port stops were soon made in Pusan Korea and then in the Philippines (the PI), specifically Subic Bay, where much deferred work was done at a much lower cost. Instead of giving the flight deck a fresh coating of non-skid before the cruise in San Diego, for example, the Navy waited till we got to the PI to do this job and thereby saved a lot of money. I'd heard a lot of stories about the Subic Bay city of Olongapo and the sin that happens there when ten thousand women come to town to meet five thousand sailors. I knew even then that this couldn't be pleasing to God. But it was the way of the world and had been for millennia.

After refitting, we headed further west and spent a few days in Singapore, thence onward through the Straight of Malacca into the Indian Ocean where we would spend the next couple months. Much of this time involved patrolling the Northern Arabian Sea with the general tasks of protecting the oil coming out of the Persian Gulf and providing a US military presence in case some Middle-East problem flared up. Now and again Arab sheiks and sultans in their superyachts would come within eyeshot of the Vinson. They liked us because we safeguarded their petrochemical gravy train.

On one fine sunny day anchored off of Oman, Captain O'Brian (he knew me as the fellow who took his daughter on a San Francisco date, got his car impounded, and woke him up at 2 a.m.) declared a steel beach picnic. Several big BBQ grills were set up on the flight deck, and each man was given a ration of two beers. Being that there was otherwise no booze on the ship, a few of the sailors were willing to pay others for their beers. Thus there were a few who became inebriated. Meanwhile, several of us musicians in the A-7 squadrons known as the Light Attack All-Stars entered the Battle of the Bands contest. I played harmonica and sang, our flight surgeon played bass, fellow pilot Brick Imerman (later to join our house in Lemoore) played guitar, and our "spy" (intelligence officer) beat the drums. Most of the bands consisted of younger enlisted fellows who played heavy metal. But we, knowing that Captain O'Brian would be judge, played songs more from his era—some Beach Boys as well as Jimmy Buffet. Thus we got fourth place, despite being somewhat deficient in talent.

The Vinson battle group not long after coming on station to protect the precious oil originally planned a port visit in Karachi, Pakistan, but just before it was to take place, the visit was cancelled because of religious riots, as I recall, in the city. That providentially played into my slow process of coming to God, as it turned out. Here's how: A week before we were to arrive in Karachi, the captain of the USS Leahy, a guided missile cruiser attached to the Vinson battle group, invited any Vinson air wing personnel who might be interested to "cross-deck" to his ship for a week and then to rejoin the carrier at the Pakistan port o' call. Always looking for something different, I volunteered. As it turned out, only two others accepted the offer: J. N. Hudson, a junior maintenance officer in our squadron, and LT Eric "Rico" Tibbets, an aviator from the VF-51 Screaming Eagles (one of two fighter squadrons aboard).

That week was an agreeable time in which we were introduced to the various facets of the "black-shoe Navy," including their excellent dining traditions. The main job of a guided missile cruiser is to protect the battle group carrier from hostile aircraft. The Leahy was essentially a floating SAM (surface to air missile) platform but had other duties as well. One day Captain Anderson—who was very hospitable—even let me take "the Con" and call out speed and compass headings while we refueled alongside a tanker. Though not at aviation levels of nerve wracking, it wasn't a walk in the park either. To keep in position took lots of concentration and ongoing calls for correction. During this time I got to know Rico pretty well, and we became friends. I don't recollect what we talked about, but he probably at least mentioned that he was a Christian.

This is where the Karachi riots come in. After a week on the Leahy, the Karachi port visit was cancelled, and they weren't able to get us back to the Vinson for yet another week. But that was more time to work on a suntan on the Leahy's deck, enjoy their five-star dining, and get to know Rico better. Having gotten to know the captain and crew better too, later they would contact me from time to time while I was airborne and request flybys. On one of those occasions (on the next cruise), I did as requested and flew fast close aboard the port (left) side. At that moment, the Leahy advised that a Soviet patrol plane was flying low level not far off the starboard side of the ship. I would have immediately gone over to escort the Russian plane, but I assumed without a second thought that he was already under escort by one or more of the Vinson fighters. Turned out he wasn't, and I was the only Vinson aircraft anywhere close. These Soviet patrol aircraft—usually used for intelligence gathering—could also sink ships and subs. When I got back aboard, the CAG (air group commander), Captain Finney, chewed me out for not escorting the Soviet plane. I apologized and told him I would have gladly, but I assumed that one of the fighters had that under control. To this day I still feel bad for not doing my duty that day.

Finally, the day came when we would start slowly making our way back home. But it would take nearly three months. Going south along the African Coast, we did some flying over Somalia and then anchored off of Mombasa Kenya and took smaller boats ashore. I obtained leave for a few days and flew up to Nairobi, rented a jeep-like truck, and drove north with some camping gear hoping to explore the Aberdare Mountains and camp out. Passing through Nyeri, I tried to find a food market with no success, but at a hardware store I was able to buy some slices of cheese as well as obtain some hardtack crackers.

While there, I suddenly heard an American female voice behind me enthusiastically exclaim, "You must be American!" She was a lady about my age, and it seemed like she hadn't seen anyone of our race or nation in quite a long time. I told her who I was, and then she told me that she was a Christian missionary based not far away and had been there for quite some time. After talking for awhile, she invited me to visit her mission station, but I politely declined, desiring more to adventure deeper into the mountains where I would camp and maybe fellowship with a baboon or two. So we parted ways. What might have been if I had gone with her and been informed of the full gospel by the flickering light of an oil lamp while the creatures of the night sang their songs by the light of the African moon? Even today, I kind of kick myself for not accepting her invitation, although she added a "seed" to the several seeds already sown.

But I was bound and determined to get around the next bend, so up I went into the clouded and rainy Aberdare Mountains. After a couple hours of uphill dirt road through dense forests, I passed a small village. Just beyond it, the road became very muddy, and the four-wheel-drive truck ground to a stop with all tires spinning. A moment later, I was surrounded by young boys from the village who, in decent English, yelled, "We push you! We push you!" I immediately agreed, and with mud flying everywhere and the twenty or so kids pushing and laughing like crazy, we got the truck another hundred yards up the road. But the mud there became hopelessly deep, so I gave up. The kids then begged me to give them a ride. So I told the oldest to organize the groups and I would take three or four at a time. The first group piled in, the rest helped me turn around, and I gave them a good ride down a ways, then back up, while squeals of delight filled the cab. Whether boys in America or Kenya, we all love trucks! Then the next group, and repeat, until finally the elder young fellow got his ride. When done, and I told him I must say goodbye (having no clue where I would go next), he looked me in the eye and said, "Thank you, thank you. May God bless you, sir." That must have touched my heart because I remember it to this day.

Going back down the mountain, I somehow found out about a rustic old hotel not far away called The Outspan, so I went there, got a room, and took a bath by the light of a candle. That night I wondered if the missionary lady was based near that village of those kids, and I also pondered the possibility that their hearts had been led to God by her words. They certainly showed God's love to me, and I sensed it, but I wasn't ready to submit to it myself. A couple days later I was back at the ship safe and sound, although in a little bit of hot water for not keeping anyone apprised of my whereabouts the last few days. Just before leaving shore I bought a bunch of wooden African animals made by the locals and ended up sending them via "Pony Express" to friends and family back home.

After Mombasa the ship headed due east, paused at the little atoll of Diego Garcia, then made a beeline toward western Australia, intending to be there by Christmas (1986). During this passage across the vast Indian Ocean, we flew, as at other times underway, maybe every second or third day. On days off we'd wear khaki uniforms and work on the things that needed to be done to run the squadron. With twelve or so jets and with about two hundred men to keep them running, there was lots to do. At this time I was "assistant personnel officer." When beginning the job I was handed a Navy Personnel (NAVPERS) standards and regulations manual that, yet again, looked like the proverbial giant family Bible. Fortunately the lead personnel officer, fellow pilot Carlos Ayuso, as well as the department chief petty officer, kept me out of trouble and pretty much told me where to sign. Later they would put me in charge of the airframe and engine maintenance divisions, which would be a little more interesting, and also make me the squadron "coffee mess officer," a job I'll describe a little later.

Just before arriving at Perth (December 19, 1986), a formation of about fifteen of our planes were sent ahead with the mission to fly over the city as low as practicable in order to alert the females amongst the indigenous population that the "Yanks" were in town. That mission was expertly accomplished and had a salutary effect. I was offered a slot in that formation, but I chose instead to do a low-level route over the red-soiled and chaparral-covered wasteland north of the city. Soon thereafter we anchored just out of the bay and proceeded ashore via Navy "Mike" boats. The city arranged a big party/dance for the battle group's officers, and many of the ladies who saw the intrepid airmen fly overhead came a-flocking.

Early in the evening my radar zeroed in on a certain Aussie lass whom I thought had an interesting exotic look. We danced away the evening, but when I asked her repeatedly if she'd like to rendezvous sometime during the next few days, she said "no," mainly because she had to work at the family farm east of town. It was almost Christmas, but for them it was summer and harvest time. When the party was over, I asked one last time, and she declined. But in all this I got a pretty good idea where her family farm was. So, rolling the dice a couple days later, I got the day off, rented a car, and after some trial and error found the farm. There was a boy standing at the entrance, and I asked him if this was where Athena[2] lived. He replied cheerfully and in the Aussie dialect, "Yeah, she's royt down theh pickin' fruit," and pointed in the direction I should go.

So I parked the car and walked down the trail and soon came upon several people picking peaches and putting them in buckets they were holding. Their backs were to me, so they didn't see me coming. One of them was obviously Athena. So when I got about fifty feet away, I gulped and hollered, "Hey, Athena, you got an extra bucket?" They all immediately turned around, and one older woman—who turned out to be Athena's mom—looked at me, then at Athena, and said, "That must be Eric!" Hearing that, I knew that I was "in there!"

Much of that day I helped the family pick and sort fruit, with regular corrections from Athena's mother regarding the latter. Athena showed me around the farm and surrounding countryside and also took me to a local animal park where you could pet the kangaroos and other marsupials. All in all she showed me a very nice time, and we expressed a common desire to see each other again some day.

On the last evening of the Vinson's Perth port o' call, I was assigned the typically boring "boat-O" (boat officer) duty. When smaller Navy boats—usually the amphibious "Mike" boats (capacity about one hundred)—took sailors between ship and shore, there had to be an officer aboard. This duty sometimes fell to the aviator officers. But this time it wasn't so *boring*. The seas, once out of the bay, were rough these couple days after Christmas, and as the evening wore on, the returning sailors appeared drunker and drunker and more rowdy. On the last boat home approaching midnight, halfway back with some water coming over the bow, all were whooping and hollering, and there were no less than three fights going on. I increasingly felt like all heck was about to break loose and they might turn on the

---

2. Pseudonym

ranking man—me—and throw him overboard if he tried to assert his authority.

Not knowing what else to do, I got up on the engine housing and started singing "Rudolf the Red-Nosed Reindeer." At first there was no effect, so I sang as loud as I could and waved my arms like a choir conductor. Then, one by one the sailors looked at me, and one fight then another stopped, and by the time we arrived at the Vinson with many onlookers gawking down in amazement, everyone on the boat was singing "Rudolf" with all the drunken gusto they could muster. Frankly, I was relieved. I still think I should have gotten a Navy Commendation Medal for going above and beyond the call of duty that night!

The next port stop was Singapore, and after that we steamed north again past Japan and Siberia up through the Aleutian Islands into the Bering Sea. The last time we were there was August. Now it was January, and proving then to the Soviets that we were fully functional that far north was a challenge. Flight operations continued, although we had to somehow get the snow and ice off the deck each morning. Several methods were tried, but the most inventive and effective was having an A-6 Intruder, with its slightly downward pointing engines, drive around the flight deck in the wee hours of the morning as the duty ice/snow blower.

The weather up there is subject to frequent low-pressure fronts that make the conditions extremely unpredictable. Thus flight operations were dicey and for the pilots risky. We all donned "poopy suits" that ostensibly would keep us dry in case we ditched or parachuted into the near-freezing ocean. But, at least for me, I suspected that these suits wouldn't do much good and would actually be an active danger if they filled up with water. As I saw it, an ejection or crash would likely not leave the suit intact. To make matters worse for myself, pulling the neck opening of the suit over my big head made the opening larger and thus made for a poor seal around my neck. Thankfully during the whole time we were up there, no one ended up in the water—although we came close. Let me explain.

One morning several aircraft were launched in not-so-bad weather, although the seas were pretty rough. When it came time to recover them, low clouds and snow blew in and it suddenly became hard to get aboard. Bubba[3] tried several times unsuccessfully in his Corsair and on his last pass came down so hard that his landing gear collapsed. Thank God, however, that he caught a wire and trapped, otherwise he would have skidded off the deck into the frigid ocean. But the problem now was that the landing area was clobbered until emergency crews could get Bubba and his crippled Corsair out of the way. For the aircrews still airborne, all they could do was circle and watch their fuel gauges go down. Apparently there were no realistic divert options. The only airfield within reach was Shemya Air Force Base near Soviet-controlled Aleutian Islands, but it was socked in and frozen over. Another pilot who was still airborne told me later that he assumed the worst and planned to radar bomb himself (i.e., eject using the radar for positioning) onto Shemya and hope that he ended up on the island rather than in the surrounding violent and freezing ocean.

Because of the ice and snow and rough seas, getting Bubba's Corsair out of the way took longer than expected. But just when things began to look really grim, a KC-130 tanker courtesy of the US Marine Corps appeared out of nowhere and offered precious fuel to those who were just about out. I don't know where he came from, but he saved the day by giving enough gas such that, despite the bad weather, all were eventually able to get back aboard. He might have been tasked to *shadow* the Vinson while we were that far north and had perhaps been on standby alert somewhere nearer the Alaskan mainland when the call for help came.

Other than some lesser tense moments before we got out of the snow zone, we arrived back in the Vinson's home port of Alameda, CA (San Francisco Bay), on February 5, 1987, in pretty good shape. Some of my squadron mates flew off back to Lemoore, but I rode the ship in. As we passed under the Golden Gate Bridge I saw people dumping what I thought was garbage on the ship from the bridge. *Those rotten war protestors,* I thought. But as the garbage hit the deck, it turned out to be hundreds of roses thrown by awaiting wives and girlfriends. Once back in Lemoore, the squadron took some days off, I went riding my dirt bike, and most of my comrades got back into family life.

---

3. Pseudonym

The next year-plus was spent in Lemoore, although toward the end of that time we started workups all over again in anticipation of going overseas again in the spring of '89. During this time Athena came to visit, and we had some excellent adventures. That summer four of us—LCDR Don "Coop" Cooper and I and our two Aussie girlfriends—drove my new Dodge Ramcharger (nicknamed "Bob") to the mountains above Fresno and then backpacked up to a high mountain lake. While I fished, the girls swam. Later that evening we sat by the fire and dined on delicious trout. The next day Athena and I climbed nearby Kaiser Peak, ten-plus thousand feet high. She was scared at times but, to her credit, persisted bravely.

About this time another event occurred that again led me to think that God was watching out for me. Four of us from the Lemoore—two couples (not Athena)—went out one day, in two 4WD trucks, to do some exploring on Black Mountain just west of town. We went up a paved road that ended at communication towers on the summit (about four thousand feet), then proceeded down a steep dirt road on the other side that terminated at the top of a very steep and deep canyon. Because I had been partaking of some wine on the drive, I didn't fully appreciate how steep the dirt road was at one spot. The road ended at the canyon edge, so we had to turn around. But when we tried going back up that really steep part, we couldn't make it.

On my third or fourth attempt, "Bob" threw a drive shaft, seemed to lose its brakes, and went out of control in a rapid acceleration downhill. To this day, it's still a mystery why I totally lost control. Because the canyon edge—nearly a cliff—was not far below, and we were hurtling toward it, I had the thought, *This is what it's like to die!* But just as we were about to fly into the abyss, Bob suddenly and miraculously ground to a lurching stop. The truck had gotten high-centered (the frame resting on the ground) right on the cliff's edge and left us literally teetering between life and death. I screamed for my lady friend to get out, and I did the same, and once clear, we stood there amazed that we had not rolled to our deaths down another thousand feet of steep canyon.

A few seconds later the grass under Bob's muffler lit on fire. As I was extinguishing that, the other couple in their stranded rig came back down the hill to help. I gingerly fetched a "come-a-long" that was stored behind Bob's front seats and with that was able to pull the truck away from the edge and onto safer ground. Then I told everyone to stay put and that I would go on foot to get help. Then I jogged back up the mountain then down the pavement eleven miles to Coalinga and made a call to my ship roommate, Chuck Meek, at about midnight. He—God bless him—drove out, found me, and we went up to rescue the rest. They had assumed I'd been eaten by a cougar or bear and were overjoyed when we showed up about 3 a.m.

A few days later, several of my squadron mates came out with multiple 4WD trucks, lots of rope and chain, and were able to get both of the stuck trucks out of the canyon. I was quite embarrassed by the whole ordeal, but I was aware that God, maybe one of His angels, had been waiting at the cliff's edge that day with a catcher's mitt and had been more merciful than I deserved.

While ashore, flying also offered some tense moments. A couple instances come to mind. After jumping over the Sierras one day, we dove down to start a canned low-level route that began at Mono Lake. There, we turned north toward the next checkpoint, Bridgeport Reservoir Dam, and separated about two miles apart into combat spread. Passing a few miles west of the ghost town Bodie at about 500 mph, I skimmed over a small ridge, and just at the moment I could see beyond it, a huge explosion suddenly appeared right in front of me, so close that to clear it I barely had time to yank the stick back, not sure if I'd hit the rising blast or not. Turned out I barely cleared it, and as I did I rocked up on a wing, looked down, and saw a fast-growing mushroom cloud just under me. It looked like a mini atomic bomb!

We had a target time at Fallon, so I kept pressing on in a bit of shock. Turned out my wingman was on the other side of a hill and never saw what happened. But I thought someone had tried to blow me out of the sky. Upon return to Lemoore I told the Navy police about the incident, and after some weeks a report came back with what had happened. The Bridgeport fire department had accumulated some years' worth of unused or confiscated fireworks and mining dynamite and blasting caps, etc., and had one day decided the best way to dispose of it all was to blow it up. So they went up on the hillside a few miles east of town, looked this way and that for any Navy jets coming through, and let 'er rip. But right when the "pickle" was pressed, I came roaring over the ridge just to the south and to their horror appeared to fly right into the massive blast.

On another occasion further south in the Owens Valley, Leon "Cowbow" Doty (he had been a rodeo rider) and I were in a dogfight when suddenly I heard a muffled bang, and immediately the cockpit temperature went from normal to broiling. Turning down the cockpit temperature knob did nothing, so after a few more panicky moments I shut down cockpit pressurization altogether. Being at about twenty thousand feet, what pressure there was immediately dumped, as did the pressure in my body with a sucking groan and wheeze. Just at the moment I started to grab the ejection handle to find relief from the roasting, the temperature abruptly reversed course and cooled down as the ambient air came in (without my oxygen mask on, I would have passed out). I didn't know then what had malfunctioned but found out later that my cockpit pressurization turbine had disintegrated and allowed raw engine to bleed air (out of the extremely hot compressor section) from the engine directly into the cockpit. The same principle applies to a home air fryer fast cooker in which large chunks of meat go from frozen to well done in short order.

The fun wasn't over yet. Thinking that my engine was coming apart, I headed immediately toward nearby NAWS (Naval Air Weapons Station) China Lake. Their airspace was normally closed due to occasional weapons testing but could be used in emergencies. By the time I raised someone there on the radio, I was pretty close in and landed safely shortly after. As I shut down the plane and began to exit, the operations officer of the base roared up in a car, jumped out, and with a look of great consternation yelled, "Do you know what just happened?!" I replied, "Yes, I just about got cooked in the cockpit like a Thanksgiving turkey!" He yelled back, "No! You just about got blown to bits by a Phoenix missile—you're lucky to be alive!"

By that time I was out of the cockpit, and he had his finger in my chest, accusing me of stupidly coming in unauthorized, and told me the rest of the story: Just as I intruded their airspace, an F-14 Tomcat had been cleared hot to shoot down an old F-86 Sabrejet drone with the gigantic and mega-deadly Phoenix missile. But his radar locked up on me instead. Just as he was going to let 'er rip, someone on the ground observing the shoot saw me appear on his radar screen near the F-86 and immediately told the Tomcat crew to abort the launch. As the Ops O told me this, the original drone target came in for an unmanned landing. From the frying pan into the fire. Yet again someone was looking out after me.

About this time I finally came of age in my father's eyes. He and Mom came by Lemoore for a brief visit just when we were beginning to prepare for the next cruise. Part of the preparation was, like times before, to do many mock carrier landings at the end of the runway. I asked and got permission to have them taken to the "carrier box" right next to the land-based Fresnel lens so they could see the action up close. Then I launched leading a flight of four and, after a slow circle over the San Juaquin Valley farm fields, came roaring in to the "break" at about 400 knots and broke downwind in succession. Then one by one we came crashing down—with a couple of our squadron LSOs coaching us—to the simulated carrier deck painted on the runway and roared off into the air to do it again. We kept this going until each of us were "bingo" on fuel. On each pass I marveled at the fact that Mom and Dad were there only a few feet away each time I hit the deck, and I assumed that with each ear-shattering pass, they would both (but Dad especially) be in a state of disbelief: *This is Eric, our son?*! That night over dinner Dad confessed that for the first time I had gained some respect in his eyes.

Not long after, we began our intermittent workups on the Vinson. By this time I felt pretty comfortable around the ship day as well as night (but I didn't dare leave my harmonica at home!), so the workups went very well. By then CDR Branch was the skipper and CDR Richard "Woolsey" Clayton the XO. Then, in the late spring, out we went and again ventured north instead of west and passed through the Aleutians without a hitch, then headed southwest along the lee of the Soviet-controlled Kuril Islands. It was somewhere near here, as I recall, that I had a brush with death.

The weather one day was crummy, so no one flew. Late that afternoon I was told to launch and look for better weather so the ship could do some flight ops that night. My mission: weather reconnaissance. So off I went into the rain and clouds and didn't see blue sky until I reached about thirty thousand feet. In all directions were clouds below and many thunderstorm heads rising above me in the distance. After going out about a hundred miles, I began to arc around the ship at that distance, but no luck; the lousy weather was everywhere. By then it was almost dark, and a little bit later the ship told me to abort the mission and get back aboard ASAP. I immediately thought about other times when I couldn't get aboard and the ship had to keep steaming into the wind and wait for me. Never again did I want to hold up the show.

With that thought I hustled to bring the airplane in. As I did, I descended back into the clouds and rushed to get all the things done that needed to be done. But now it was night, the rain was hitting the windscreen hard, and bursts of light from lightning were coming at a regular pace. I perceived that things were happening too fast, and as a result I was "getting behind the airplane." In the rush I started making little mistakes. For one thing, I forgot to play my harmonica. About ten miles out, but without the ship in sight because of the rain and clouds, and not sure about the ship's heading, I was told to switch radio frequency.

With some vertigo setting in and still rushing to get all checks complete, I switched over and immediately heard the LSOs say that they had me on radar and to "keep it coming." Today I don't recall the specific LSO calls except the last, but I do know that from two miles to one mile to close in, there were lots of calls as they finally got me in sight, and the whole time I couldn't see a thing. With the hard rain and vertigo, it was an extremely nerve-wracking thing to see the radar altimeter go from five hundred to four hundred to three hundred to two hundred while not seeing the ship at all—just rain-deluged blackness punctuated by blinding flashes of lightning. But I trusted them and, in faith, kept it coming, believing at any moment I would at last see the lights of the landing zone and the meatball and get aboard. But I was as fearful and wound up tight as I'd ever been in my life.

Passing what was about one hundred feet, a different voice than had been talking me down suddenly screamed "WAVE OFF! WAVE OFF! WAVE OFF!" and kept it up until I had slammed the throttle forward and climbed. Approach control, who monitored the frequency, told me to switch to another frequency, and they guided me around for another pass—this time with a long straight in setup. I might have even asked for more time to get my act together because my nerves by then were completely shot. On that approach I still didn't see the ship when the LSOs started talking me down, but at some point I did get sight of the ship and was able to get aboard.

The LSOs, including the CAG (Carrier Air Group) LSO, were waiting in the ready room when I finally got there. The CAG LSO, soaked and visibly upset, said with deadly seriousness, "Do you know that you almost flew into the water tonight?" Dumbfounded, I replied, "No," and asked him what he meant. He then went on to recount how as they were talking down an A-6 tanker, he had noticed out of the corner of his eye through the rain sweeping over the deck a faint light that was descending toward the ocean about a mile away on the opposite side of the ship. Seeing the light just about to impact the water, and not sure what it was, he let go with the screaming "WAVE IT OFF!" calls. When he said this, my jaw dropped as I realized that I was not, in fact, the only plane airborne that night.

As we talked a little further, it dawned on us that I had somehow in the stormy confusion wound up doing a simultaneous final approach to the ship with the A-6 tanker, and that believing that I was the only plane airborne that night, the LSO calls given to *him* I took to be for *myself*. When they said, "You're high," I pulled power. When they said, "Right for lineup," I pulled the stick to the right. When they said, "You're working slow," I added power, etc. In reality, though, I was going further and further off course and ever closer to the invisible ocean. If the CAG LSO had not seen me in his peripheral vision that night, I would have flown into Davy Jones's Locker and disappeared without a trace. As I later pondered all this on my bunk, still trembling, I had a burning realization that God had mercifully spared me that night.

A few days later we did some flying over islands just off the Japanese mainland. Looking down under cloudy foreboding skies, the sea everywhere was rough and foamy, and the dark volcanic islands in places had smoke emitting from them. I recall thinking that it was no surprise that Godzilla came from a place like this. We also flew a low level one day over South Korea and, if I remember right, bombed one of their targets. Not long after we again came to Subic Bay where we spent an extended time getting the ship up to snuff. I had recently been assigned (in addition to other duties) the coffee mess officer job, thus I had to make hay while I could in the Philippines.

Now one might think, *What does coffee have to do with "making hay" in the Philippines?* Well, grab a cup o' joe, light the smoking lamp, take a seat, and let me explain. When in the various ports during cruise, the squadron officers have need of hotel rooms, beer, booze, and snacks. All that costs money and sometimes a lot of it depending on the port and rate of consumption. Enter the coffee mess officer—a job no one wants yet a job that has more effect on squadron happiness than perhaps any other. With the Chargers, this man's duty was, yes of course, to keep the ready room coffee mess supplied so that the aviators—but especially the skipper and XO (or even the CAG or the admiral if they came by)—would have easy access to hot coffee as well as associated sugar and non-dairy whitener (no mochas or lattes in those days). But far more important than that was the duty to raise money sufficient to have world-class admins in port supplied with the finest of beverages and goodies. This was the much harder part of the job, but due to my previous pack-minus performance, I was hand-selected as the officer most likely to achieve success in this critical mission. The skipper chose wisely, and indeed, success we had. Now back to the Philippines.

As soon as the ship docked in Subic Bay, I had to rush off in order to begin the process of ordering items that we would sell to the ship's crew while underway during the next few months. These sales would fund "the mess." I already had in mind and had designed what to get; all I needed was for the very industrious Filipinos to make it for me. This included ball caps, T-shirts, sweatshirts, etc., and, yes, even ladies' panties—all of these with the VA-27 Chargers logo on them and, in some cases, an image of an A-7 embroidered in. I managed within a day to barter prices, make contracts, and give down payments, usually with my own money. Then, all we could do was wait and hope that all arrived at the dock before the ship lifted the gangplank and headed for points further west.

Everything came in with plenty of time, except the panties. So we waited and waited until it was the morning we were to leave. So I called the proprietor of the company, one Mr. J. Ong, and he assured me they were on the way. Again we waited. Not more than ten minutes before drop-dead time, up he drove in his station wagon. He pushed a couple of big boxes out the back and sped away before we could talk. We hauled the boxes up to the ship, and when we got a chance to open them we found that all was in order except the panties had this embroidery: "VA-27 Chargeks." The land of not quite right. These were discounted but actually sold quite well to the sailors who wanted to send something nice—not necessarily perfect—to their loves back home.

From there we went to Singapore again. What an immaculately clean city, and the seafood offerings were out of sight. Biggest prawns I'd ever seen! After a couple days there, I was flown to Butterworth Royal Malaysian Air Force Base in a Navy transport aircraft. Meanwhile the Carl Vinson left port and steamed up the western coast of the Malay Peninsula. That night, Malaysian fighter pilots took me out on the town of Penang, where we had a great time.

Very early the next morning I climbed into a Malaysian Air Force helicopter (old French-made "Alouette") and took off. I wanted to doze off, being quite hung over, but the non-English-speaking pilot motioned for me with a smile to take the controls (pilot and co-pilot each had their own set of controls). I cautiously did so, flying the contraption all the way out to the target island where the Vinson aviators would soon bomb and strafe. I was to be the range safety officer. Everything jiggled in the little helo, including all my innards. Instead of one stick like I was used to, there were two sticks that the piloting pilot had to deal with, and instead of the throttle being conveniently located on the left console like in every other airplane in the whole world, that French machine had the throttle on the end of one of the two sticks, and it had to be twisted like a motorcycle throttle grip.

Flying the shaking machine was like the proverbial chewing gum and rubbing your belly and doing the hula hoop on the back of a shaking hippo all at the same time. The whole ride out, I thought at any moment the machine would shake itself apart, and, having no ejection seat or parachute, we'd be goners. The host pilot said nothing the entire time but just pointed the way with a Buddha-like smile. After an hour or so, he pointed ahead to a little island where we were supposed to land. So I moved one stick one way, the other stick the other way, and untwisted the throttle and began a slow decent. I didn't at first see where to land, but as he kept pointing I finally picked out the little landing pad next to a lovely lagoon. With him continuing to point and smile, I came down lower and lower until I was right over the landing pad at about thirty feet. I was quite proud of myself. Problem was, I was still doing about 100 mph. I didn't know how to slow the thing down! So I climbed back up, looked at him, smiled, and motioned for him to retake the controls. I didn't want to kill us both. He did a crop duster turn, and a few moments later we were perfectly settled on the landing pad.

The Vinson air wing bombers and fighters started showing up about an hour later. Chargers, Warhawks, Nightriders, Screaming Eagles, and Sundowners would check in, and I'd make sure the range was clear and clear them in "hot." There really wasn't much of a range, but only a plywood deck about ten-by-ten feet floating out in the middle of the lagoon a quarter mile from our observation post. The strafing was real, but all the bombs that day were the little twenty-five-pound "blue death" that we often used instead of more expensive life-sized bombs.

It all got a bit boring after awhile, although there was one pass made by one of the Knightriders (flying an A-6 Intruder) that got our attention. I had dropped hundreds of those little bomblets before, and occasionally on a low-level fast delivery the bomb would hit the water, dive, then porpoise out of the water and dive again to disappear. You would know its initial impact point because a puff of smoke would appear there (from a charge in the bomb's nose, which could be seen as a flash of light at night). The Knightrider came in fast on a typical low altitude and low angle run. I cleared him hot, and he released the bomb. It hit the water well short of the target, dove, then came flying out of the water still doing 300 mph-plus down range, then dove back in the water and again zoomed out of the water now doing about 200, arced back into the lagoon and, to my utter amazement, flew out of the water a third time going almost straight up and landed KAPLUNK on top of the plywood bullseye! To make sure my eyes weren't fooling me, I grabbed a pair of binoculars, and sure enough, that bomb was sitting right in the middle of the bullseye platform amidst several holes from other bombs and bullets that had passed through.

After everyone went home, I had my comrade—the helo pilot—row me out to the bullseye where I retrieved the bomb. Its tail was horribly bent but was otherwise in good shape. We then packed up and flew back to Butterworth. Once I got back to the ship on a Navy carrier onboard delivery (COD) transport plane, I went to the Knightrider ready room and presented the bomb to the pilot who dropped it and told him the story. On the range I had called the drop something like "three hundred feet at six o'clock" but now told him that this was corrected to a "bullseye"!

Unlike Malaysia, not many nations provided us places to practice bombing and strafing. So most of the time we had to make our own targets and be happy with that. A typical day's flight during cruise would find us loaded with those dreaded "blue death" bomblets just described and a magazine full of twenty-millimeter ammo. Usually as a flight of two, we would get fired off the catapult and stay close to the water for at least fifty miles. This served to make it harder for Soviet aircraft or ships using radar to find us. We didn't want to be like a swarm of bees right above the hive. Then we'd climb out and go about a hundred miles away from the ship, drop a flare or two in the water that would produce smoke at day and a bright light at night, and then circle around at varying altitudes and bomb and/or strafe it. That completed, we'd go to Indian Country and hone our dogfighting skills with anyone we encountered there, or we'd just turn on each other like rabid dogs and (simulated) try to shoot each other down. For a real treat, the ship from time to time would tow a spar about a thousand feet astern. This device made a wake that we could bomb and strafe from a pattern round about the ship. This was fun for us and was also quite a show for the sailors on deck. The problem was that despite instructions not to aim at the spar but at the wake behind it, the tow cable would nevertheless routinely be cut by a bullet or bomb, and that would end the fun for the day.

The Philippines, on the other hand, let us use several bombing ranges. One was just off the coast, a big rock that jutted out of the seafloor. The rock was always surrounded by Bangka boats manned by divers who would swim down and retrieve the dummy bombs. Therefore the procedure was to buzz the boats first so they could clear out at a safe distance, then do our business. When we left, the boats would rush back in, and the salvage diving would begin in earnest. The scuttlebutt was that by the time you got to Olongapo a few days later, they'd have pots and pans and squadron belt buckles already available all made from those same bombs. Speaking of that, not long before I joined the Chargers, one of the pilots crashed and died in the jungle not too far from Subic Bay. When rescue crews finally got there a day or two later, not much of the wreckage remained. Most pieces had already been scavenged by the native *Negritos* and other locals and brought to town for remanufacture and resale. The chief who worked with me at the time had to go into the jungle in order to disarm what remained of the ejection seat. It was a horrible task, but someone had to do it.

Occasionally we'd join other air wing aircraft in a bigger "war at sea" exercise or simulated "alpha strike," with fighter escort and all. On one of those, one of the Warhawk pilots got in a "crack the whip" contest with a KC-10 refueling hose and left his probe in the basket, which meant a scrub for the mission. On another occasion they somehow found an actual boat—something like an old tuna trawler—to sink. The mission was to come in low and fast. So I, along with my wingman, did just that, popped up, and saw nothing. Even after I climbed up to look around, I never got sight of it. I was pretty embarrassed when I got back and debriefed with the skipper.

One of those big alpha strike missions was the longest and most painful flight of my Navy experience. It involved another case of mortal combat with the relief tube. In an earlier awkward event, I flew for some time with the quart-size funnel brimming because I didn't know how to drain it. In this case, there was a malfunction. We all launched, rendezvoused, and headed out on a long mission that involved multiple refuelings. About an hour into the mission I needed relief, so I picked up the funnel and, as was my regular practice after the first incident, tested it. I spit in the funnel, looked down into the bottom, and pressed the magic button at the base to make sure the fluid would exit. This time the spitball didn't budge. So I repeated the test, but no luck. *Oh no.* After fiddling around with it for some time, I came to the stark realization that there would be no relief at all on what I knew to be probably the longest mission of my Navy career. *Could I do it, or would I earn an even worse call sign?*

After another hour or so, things began to get painful. So I employed everything I could find that had a cavity and was sealable, including a flashlight after the D cell batteries were removed. Having done that, there were no other options except one that I refused to take. The only thing to do was gut it out. Flying and refueling (which takes intense concentration) and bombing all in coordination with many other machines is a challenge on the best of days. This was far from the best of days.

By and by, we finally headed back to the ship. By the time it came into sight, my innards were at red alert, and all I could think about was the flight deck urinal on the side of the ship's island. When my turn to trap finally came, I had a laser focus on that meatball like never before. I wasn't about to bolter or get waved off. When the hook caught and I slammed forward in the straps, I thought my lower abdomen would rupture for sure, yet I was overjoyed to be back home. The normally quick process of getting parked and shut down seemed to take an eternity. At last, I climbed down from the cockpit, threw the defiled items overboard, and staggered over to the island.

Many days, as before, were spent up in the northern Arabian Sea, twiddling our thumbs and waiting for something interesting to happen. That day finally came—well, actually night—and it was pretty much a fizzle, although it portended for me more what I was to do in the second half of my life. By this time CDR Clayton had become the CO and CDR Stan "Quila" Hlavka the XO.

That evening we were to blast off, head up into the Straight of Hormuz that leads to the Persian Gulf, and shoot up Iranian "Boghammer" gunboats that intelligence expected to harass oil-laden tankers that night. I was pretty stoked, although I wondered how we would see gunboats (glorified motorboats) at night. The A-7 had a targeting radar, but about all you could see with it were supertankers, aircraft carriers, peninsulas, and such. But motorboats?

Then the word came down: "Bhagwan, you're flying tonight—but in the tanker." There must have been some devious logic with the schedulers: "Hey, we're protecting tankers tonight from Boghammers, so let's put Bhagwan in the tanker!" I ask the reader to bear with me for a moment as I digress regarding the A-7's tanker mission.

All during cruise, one of our jets was kept in a tanker configuration (sometimes two jets), meaning, instead of bombs it carried an extra fuel tank and a "buddy store" from Vietnam War vintage out of which came a forty-or-so-feet-long hose. At the end of the hose was a drogue or basket in which another aviator in another jet could place his probe and receive precious aviation fuel (which is much like stove oil or diesel fuel). The oil that we were there to protect coming through the Straight of Hormuz went on via supertanker to the US and was processed, and a little of it was put onboard the Carl Vinson, then put in our airplanes so we could protect the oil coming out and keep the cycle going.

Anyway, the pilots were generally lukewarm about the tanker mission because it mostly involved doing endless circles in the sky, waiting for someone to get in a jam. Each launch had a duty tanker, sometimes one of us, or one of the Warhawks, or one of the Knightriders in an A-6. The duty tanker's job was a standby job: if someone had trouble getting aboard, or there were problems on the ship and recovery had to be delayed, planes getting low on fuel could hit the duty tanker. Sometimes fuel was scheduled to go to certain aircraft that were on a mission that required more fuel. These were usually the fighters because they had afterburners, and they used them a lot while dogfighting. Especially for them, but for us too, the more fuel you had, the more fun you could have. So, just like anyone else who has a highly desired commodity (like gold, silver, money, power tools, hamburgers, cookies, etc.), you'll inevitably have moochers who will try to get you to share. So it was as the tanker driver. Sometimes someone, usually a Screaming Eagle or Sundowner Tomcat, would simply show up out of nowhere, and the pilot and back-seat RIO would stare at me. If I didn't let my hose out, he'd soon disappear like a ghost. If I put the hose out, he'd plug in, and I'd give him a little top-off. Sometimes they would radio me on a discreet frequency and beg for even just a little bit. Rico was the biggest mooch of all, but because he was by then a friend, I did what I could.

In reality, those "buddy stores" were horribly unreliable, so even if I wanted to give liberally, one element or another of the system wouldn't work. The mission was especially difficult at night because, among the usual aviating challenges, the pilot's oxygen and G-suit hoses lay right over the buddy store control panel, and, to make matters worse, the panel was furthest aft and unlit. There weren't enough hands to fly and lift up the hoses and hold a flashlight and do the switchology all at the same time. To add insult to injury, the switch that started the transfer of fuel was identical and right next to the switch that retracted the hose. At night in bad weather, some poor aviator with dwindling fuel would struggle for many minutes trying to get plugged in, and when at last successful, his joy would turn to dismay when the tanker pilot hit the wrong switch and sucked the basket off his probe.

I recall one buddy store malfunction that was interesting. At the end of a tanker cycle, I refueled another jet, but when I tried to retract the hose, nothing happened. So I tried this and that—no joy. After exhausting my knowledge up there, I called operations on the ship where squadron mates hung out if help was needed. They offered a few suggestions that didn't work then, as a last resort, told me to hit the buddy store's *guillotine* button, which would slice off the hose. So I did that, but nothing happened. Someone then suggested that I speed up as fast as I could go and see if the hose would stretch and snap off. So I climbed up, sped up, and went into a dive, with the machmeter showing near supersonic. Nothing—except the hose got a lot longer and the basket, which weighed about a hundred pounds, was still attached.

It's interesting that, as far as I recall, no one ever suggested just jettisoning the buddy store, which I think I could have done. But those ancient buddy stores were precious, far more precious than the fuel that they transferred. At last the air boss said to just come back aboard and hope for the best. So that's what I did. My only concern was that the drogue might fly up and over the jet when I trapped and conk me over the head. As it turned out, the drogue, now back about seventy-five feet, hit the deck a moment before the plane, impacted one of the arresting wires, broke off, and went whizzing past the meatball into the ocean. Otherwise, all was good.

Now back to the Iranian *Boghammers*. This involved only one evening launch, and I took my place over the ship, waiting for anyone who might need some fuel. Meanwhile the armed aircraft headed north up into the Straight of Hormuz but, as I recall now, didn't find any gunboats harassing any tankers. I did get a little "action" that night, though. Toward the end of the two-hour cycle, one of my squadron mates radioed me, told me he was short of fuel, and asked me to meet him as soon as possible. So I headed north, and we found each other about a hundred miles from the ship. After a tricky rendezvous, he got plugged in and, thankfully, the buddy store worked and transferred the precious fuel. Recovery for all was uneventful. So there you have it. My only night of "combat"—and it officially wasn't even that for me because I didn't enter the "combat zone" well north of the ship.

Thinking about this now, it reminds me of that test that I took at the end of high school that was intended to indicate a suitable vocation. Then, I wanted to be a fighter pilot, but they said I'd make a better "nurse." There in the Northern Arabian Sea that night at the tip of the American naval sword, all the previous training to be a destroying killer was funneled down to one brief moment of *nursing*. Oh, the marvelous ironies of life!

The dog days of the Arabian Sea late summer dragged on. Our little squadron band—the Light Attack All-Stars—broke the monotony now and then by performing popular songs for the sailors on the mess deck, and there on some evenings I'd do my coffee mess duty and sell our squadron offerings. We also did some flying here and there when not anchored off Oman with the sultan's yacht nearby. The sultan of that state did graciously allow us to do some flying over his sultanate. These flights usually consisted of a low-level ending in a thrilling dive down Star Wars Canyon, which led out to the sea. On one of those flights by myself, cruising over the endless desert at low level, not seeing anything but sand, I was amazed at a sight that flashed by the starboard side. The scene reminded me somewhat of the cows and cowboy I had seen in Nevada some years before. This time, however, it was about twenty or so goats, and standing amongst them was a woman with a shepherd's staff dressed head to toe in a black burqa. She and her goats were all alone in the vast boiling desert wasteland. From time to time I still think about her, who she was, what her life was like, and what she thought when I flew by. Americans have little idea of just how primitive much of the world still is and, I might say, the level of subjugation that much of the Muslim world imposes upon their women where there is not much western influence.

Before we finally left our duty post in the North Arabian Sea, a fluke of circumstances almost put me into said Sea. As I was heading out of the ready room one very hot day to get suited up and head topside for a flight, the duty officer said, "Hey, Bags. Flight Deck just called and said you now have four Mark 84s on your plane." Apparently an A-6—a much bigger aircraft—that had originally been loaded with those bombs had a mechanical problem, but Flight Deck didn't want to take the bombs back below, so they put them on my jet and told me to just get rid of them. So as I put my gear on and went up to do the preflight, it went through my mind that instead of the almost weightless blue death bombs, I now had eight thousand pounds of real bombs—*far more* weight than I'd ever carried.

Getting up to the catapult was like trying to taxi a loaded dump truck. When I at last got sent down the cat, it seemed for the weight to be a bit weak, and as soon as I reached the ship's edge, my mighty corsair, despite being at full power, immediately started settling toward the water. My good friend Pat "Gunz" Walters, who had loaded up the bombs, worriedly watched the catapult sequence, intently aware of the extremely heavy load. When he saw me disappear below the deck right off the cat, he thought that any moment he'd either see me jettison the load, eject, or crash. Happily, after several seconds, with some deft airmanship on the edge of stall, I did begin a very slow climb. Gunz was overjoyed when he saw me reappear. That crisis over, I radioed the air boss and told him that I thought the cat shot had been a bit weak. That call would, by day's end, come back to bite me in an ironic way.

Once well away from the ship in open ocean, I dropped the bombs one by one. What an awesome sight—each one sending up a geyser as tall as the Empire State Building! When I got back aboard and to the ready room, it became immediately apparent that I was in some kind of hot water. Turns out that my call about the soft cat shot set in motion a cascade of pointing fingers. The ship's engineering department said all parameters were correct for my cat shot and that there had been no malfunction. Thus the problem must be on the aviation side. The air wing and then the squadron leaders, while I was still gone watching sky scrapers go up, went to the complex graphs at the back of the A-7 Operations Manual (some I never recall using) and calculated that, given the extreme load, hot temperature, air density, humidity level, tilt of the earth, magnetic variation, level of cosmic background radiation, and perhaps other factors, my Corsair that day would in fact *not fly*. They dinged me for taking the jet, but I think the skipper took most of the heat. Maybe God gave me a little *lift* that day, and/or maybe He moved the aeronautics engineers at Vought to factor in a little slop in their charts in order to give a little live-saving padding to bumbling aviators like me.

At last our tour of oil-defending duty ended, and we, like the time before, headed south to Mombasa. Knowing next to nothing about what I was getting into, I talked three buddies—Rico, Steve Molter, and Scott Weller—into trying to climb Mt. Kenya. They naively agreed, so we took a Kenya Airways flight to Nairobi, then found someone at the airport to fly us closer to the mountain. After a night at the Naro Moro River Lodge, we hired some porters, but the money they wanted was, in my mind, crazy high. I didn't realize that the Lodge was a good twenty miles from the top of the mountain, that it was the rainy season, and that to get near the top would involve an elevation gain of some ten thousand feet. Recall that in those days we did not have internet or cell phones, and the only communication means possible was through mail service that took weeks going back and forth between ship and shore. In other words, any communication with persons in Kenya was impossible. Thus, when I came up with the idea of climbing Mt. Kenya, there was no way to get information or make any reservations in advance.

So it was, in hindsight, kind of a miracle that we got as far as we did and actually started the expedition toward the second-highest mountain in Africa (behind Kilimanjaro). For several hours we trudged up the muddy path in the steaming jungle as rain came down continually. Because of the cost of the porters (I tried to bargain, but they wouldn't budge), and because it was then dawning on me that I was probably getting us in over our heads and that the rain would at some point turn to snow, I quickly lost heart yet insisted that we go on. Only much later did I learn that the last three thousand feet or so of Mt. Kenya consists of volcanic towers that are seriously steep and require serious climbing equipment. In other words, in ignorance and bravado, I was getting us into a danger zone out of which one or more of us might not emerge.

But once again, providence brought along a circumstance that most likely averted further folly. Late in the day, with everyone tired and soaked, giant hairy monkeys—two-thirds the size of gorillas—suddenly appeared in the trees all around and glared at us menacingly. That sight alone alarmed us. But when we tried to go on into their territory, they started warning us with earsplitting *barks* (for the lack of a better word) that unnerved us. With each horrible bark, a cloud of steam would come flying out of their mouths. That's when I agreed, along with the others, to throw in the towel and head back to the Lodge where dry clothes and hot food could be ours, and we wouldn't be eaten by angry barking mega-monkeys.

This was kind of a relief for my friends—and me too, but I was crestfallen and quite embarrassed that the mission didn't succeed. For the next couple days we sat around the little lodge, and I did some fishing in the nearby creek. We also visited the posh Mount Kenya Safari Club one day and, according to a recollection of Rico, met and chatted there with a lady who was related to the archaeologist Louis Leakey.

Again we hired a small plane to fly us back to Nairobi. This time the pilot flew quite low over the eastern slope of the red-soiled Aberdare Mountains where a couple years before I had gotten stuck and given the village kids a ride. We got back to Mombasa just fine. At the dock, I asked several of the wooden carving vendors if they could sell me something for the few leftover shillings in my pocket.

One of them agreed and handed me a rather evil-looking carved image—something like an angry god or demon—and with that I headed for the local boats that took sailors back and forth to the ship anchored in the bay. Coming around the corner of a house, a big raven looking down at me from the eave started cawing. This seemed ominous. Then as I came in sight of the dock, there was a hubbub going on, and I was told that a native man had just been crushed to death between the dock and one of the boats. Being somewhat superstitious, I promptly took the carved image that seemed to be bringing on this bad jambo back to the man who sold it to me, got half my money back, then returned to the dock with my conscience clear and finally made passage back to the mother ship.

A couple weeks later, going ashore at the little atoll of Diego Garcia was delayed because the visiting admiral in charge of the Indian Ocean area decided that our ship looked like a "garbage scow." Once set free, I played my harmonica that night with a newly formed Navy rock band who knew only a few songs. Instead of repeating songs, we just jammed as the sunset glow faded and the lagoon waters lapped nearby. A few weeks after that, the ship anchored off Pattaya Beach, Thailand, and we took smaller local boats as close to shore as possible and waded from there. Rico flew his fiancée, Mitzie, over, and I met up with them in Bangkok at the US Embassy as they applied for a marriage license and I for a new passport. A day or two later many of us attended their wedding at the base of a huge ancient Buddhist pagoda. It was a splendid affair. Not long after, I and Charger comrade Dave "Weed" Kolarik went up against two Screaming Eagle fighters, Rico being one of them. Two Corsairs vs. two Tomcats. Who won? I thought we did; they debriefed a different picture. God knows. At very least, for a couple of Light Attack bubbas, we gave 'em a pretty good run for their money!

On the way back to the States, we yet again made port at the PI. There, on Skipper CDR Clayton's orders, I helped arrange for a cruise board to be made. This was speedily accomplished, and before we left port, the completed item was given to the Cubi Point Officers' Club (at Subic Bay) to hang on their wall. The board, about five feet square, was made of some exotic Filipino wood. It had the names of all the Charger aviators on that cruise carved into it, and there was a Corsair II bursting out of the top of the board. Some years later when the Philippines president threw out the Yanks just after Mt. Pinatubo exploded, they packed up the Cubi O'Club nearly as is and transferred it to the Naval Aviation Museum in Pensacola, FL. Last time I was there (2017), I spotted that same VA-27 Chargers cruise board hanging from the ceiling. My last memory of the real Cubi O'Club was an impromptu wrestle-a-thon that went down the last night there. A few beers transformed me into a rainbow, and I was able to hold my own. But by the time we got back to the ship, I was skinned up, hung over, sore, and back to my usual cutthroat self.

Instead of going far north on the way back, this time we went via Hawaii and stayed for a few days. Coffee mess sales during the cruise had gone very well, so we got a lovely room at the Waikiki Hilton. Hundreds of male relatives poured into town, including my nephew Dan, and when we left there to head directly home, they were onboard—a privilege the Navy called a "tiger cruise." The "tigers" got to see the ship and flight operations in all their glory.

Almost three years before when I was first on the Vinson, my father had come on a short tiger cruise out of San Diego and had been amazed by what he saw. Now it was Dan's turn to be amazed—not just by the flying but by the city under the flight deck. He also helped me in hauling music equipment to and from the mess deck when we did our little concerts there. During that last week on the ship we had to unload as much of the squadron "geedunk" as possible, so Dan assisted with sales and the last of the items were discounted and sold. On the fly off back to Lemoore, I took some photos of our sister squadron, the Warhawks, flying past the ship, then with one last look at the Vinson myself, bid farewell and came back ashore for good.

Between the workups and cruises of the last three years, there had been some cost to man and machine. Regarding the latter: An A-6 of the Knightriders was lost at sea (see next paragraph). Two Tomcats at different times were lost when they ended up in spins and could not recover. The crews successfully ejected and were rescued out of the deep. In both cases the front seat pilots looked like Godzilla upon returning to the ship. The pilot in a spinning F-14 is a good fifteen feet forward of the axis of spin, thus experiences extreme "eyeballs out" centrifugal force, and so the whites of the eyes fill with blood. Hence the Godzilla look. Another Tomcat later went over the side at night when the arresting cable broke. Both crewmen ejected successfully, one ending up on the deck, the other in the water. The Chargers, on flyout from Lemoore to the ship, lost an A-7 when a wing folded. The pilot (who, as I recall, was the CAG LSO who saved my life) was roughed up in the ejection but survived. A Warhawk A-7 lost braking ability and went over the side. The pilot ejected and was plucked a little later from the water unscathed. Another Warhawk A-7's tail was destroyed on the hanger deck when one of the giant divisional doors closed and crushed it. A wave had swept over the nearby lowered elevator and hit a box which in turn fell on the button that closed the divisional door.

Regarding man: One of my friends and a best-liked fellow on the ship died in a non-service-related accident. When we were in port San Diego (where he was stationed when ashore), he had taken me up in his tail-dragging bush plane, and we had a blast flying through the local mountains and down a deep canyon where the railroad used to run. He invited me to fly to Mexico with him soon after, but I was unable due to other commitments. Sadly, he died on that trip when his airplane hit a mountainside. At sea, an A-6 Intruder went out of control at night. The BN got out OK, but the pilot (who first taught me the tanker concept of being checked "sweet") perished. Finally, a couple of my squadron mates one day came down from the crow's nest in torment of heart because they had just seen one of the deck sailors blown into the JBD and overboard by one of the jets at full power on the catapult. He was soon fished out of the water, but his life was gone. For a ship with five thousand men doing ongoing dangerous operations, we were fortunate to lose so few.

Our return from cruise was mid-December 1988, and I only had a couple months to go in the squadron. Overall it had been a great time, despite the challenges and close calls, and the men I worked with were in nearly all cases a blessing. A few ups and downs during my last few months with the Chargers might here be mentioned.

As I said before, I was a better pilot than officer. Throughout my time in the Navy I found it hard to do the officer duties because, first, I had a hard time getting my head around all that was required, and second, I had an ongoing sense of mild insecurity when it came to relating to those above me in rank. Those who do well are men who can keep on top of the paperwork and feel secure enough around their superiors that they can develop a bond with them and even show a little love through loyalty. In my Christian life I've gotten a little better at this, but even today it still bums me out how imperfect I am in this regard. Anyway, just before leaving the squadron I got a pretty sub-standard "fitness report." It doesn't take much tomfoolery to get knocked below others, and I had my share while with the Chargers. A few instances, among others, certainly didn't help.

One day at sea I received a care package from someone back home. I opened the box in the ready room, with a few others looking on, and saw within the box several small cans of Margarita drinks, each having some small amount of tequila within. Consumption of alcohol on the ship other than the once-a-cruise ration mentioned previously was forbidden. One or two other squadrons were pretty loose regarding this, but ours took a hard line. It was late in the cruise, however, so I didn't think it was a big deal. The box was taken to my room and consumed. The story is a little complicated from there, but it is enough to say that I got in some hot water for that, and a related issue made it more problematic than it otherwise would have been.

Then there was a case of piloting error followed by intentional disregard of procedures that I was forced to confess. Returning from a cross-country flight, I stopped at Holloman AFB in New Mexico to refuel late in the day. When I restarted after getting fuel, the engine died a few seconds later. Turned out I had forgotten to turn the fuel master lever on. In such cases the book said that a fuel system inspection was required to make sure no fuel hoses had collapsed. But such an inspection would mean I couldn't get back to Lemoore NAS before closing; thus I'd have to reveal my error to the skipper, and he wouldn't be happy. So, thinking that a hose collapse would be very unlikely, I turned the fuel master on, fired back up, and taxied to the runway.

When I got there, I noticed that one of the wing tanks was not transferring to the main tank like it should. I had never encountered such in the past (and never would in the future), and it didn't seem to be anything related to my original error which would involve only the fuel line between the main tank and engine. So I tried cycling pumps and circuit breakers and even sat at the end of the runway for a good twenty minutes waiting for a good transfer, but it never came. I pondered taking off anyway, but I was already guilty of two errors, and it already seemed like God was forcing my hand. Nevertheless I still contemplated going for it, but then I realized that if the wing tank didn't transfer, the plane's lateral controllability might be compromised, and, in any case, I wouldn't have enough fuel to get home. During those twenty minutes the evil one was on one shoulder, and an angel of God was on the other. Fortunately, after quite a struggle, I surrendered to the latter and figured that he was accomplishing two things: confession and disaster avoidance. So I threw in the towel, ate crow, and called the skipper once I got to the BOQ for the night and told him the whole story.

The next morning an inspection of the fuel lines was made, with no problems noted, and when I went to take off, the fuel was transferring just fine. Right then I had the strong impression that the previous night's problem had been of supernatural origin. Once back in Lemoore, the skipper had me tell the embarrassing story from A to Z to a gathering of the aviators. It was hard to take but good for my soul. God did not let me get away with the deception, and He might have saved the airplane and me in the process.

One other thing that didn't help was badmouthing one of the department heads one day inadvertently in his hearing. Again, God did not let me get away with an offense. As I sat at the Lemoore duty desk expressing negative thoughts about this man (which, in hindsight, were quite unfair), I looked down and to my horror saw the edge of the metal-framed message board lying on the squadron common frequency transmit button. I had wondered why no one had lately called in. When I lifted the board off the transmitter, this same man's voice as well as others who were out flying immediately burst forth with much cursing and yelling for me to get off the radio. When he returned from the flight he rightly was not happy at all, and the word got out that I was, at least that day, quite a jerk.

For these and other reasons, the CO's fitness report (FitRep) debrief was disappointing. Being a senior JO (junior officer) by that time, I should have done a lot better. But the reality of the bigger picture was hinted at when Skipper Clayton, right after the debrief, ordered me to take an airplane and go flying. I wasn't on the flight schedule that day. He had compassion and knew exactly what would cheer me up. I immediately took this as his way of saying that I was still an honored member of his round table.

The last days with the Chargers were really fine, and we even had enough coffee mess money left over to fund a squadron weekend of skiing at Shaver Lake in the nearby mountains. We laid out a treasure hunt for those who drove up and at the final stop sent the couples flying down a snowy slope on inflated tractor inner tubes with glasses (plastic!) of champagne in their hands. My farewell occurred then, and I told everyone what a great time it had been and wished them well. Then I was off to the VFA-127 Cylons in Fallon, NV. I had "rushed" the Cylons previously because they were in Fallon and because there was an "F" in their "VFA" designation!

6

Cowboys and Indians and Surrender to Christ

During the three-plus years flying A-7s, we had used the NAS Fallon bombing ranges many times and had also been on several air wing detachments there as we prepared for overseas deployments. On those detachments, the air wing flew large-scale mock bombing missions with fighter cover, and the Top Gun (Navy fighter weapons school) boys assisted by the Cylons tried to shoot us down. I even brought my dirt bike along once or twice. The town was like the Wild West, the flying was all "cowboys and Indians," and there were endless desolate mountains and valleys to fly over and explore. So I really politicked to get there, and that's what I got!

LCDR Len "Peewee" Fox had just arrived there, so he and I and another Cylon pilot, Ron "Ramjet" Ramsay, rented a house together. Not long after, the house was sold, which got my goat. But I remember Peewee saying, "Don't worry, I've always fallen off the pony into a bed of clover." And, by golly, so it was! A man a little down the road, Mr. Bud Ernst, heard about us and offered to rent us his beautiful ranch home. Even though Bud's large feed lot was only a stone's throw away; thus the place often had a fragrant odor, I couldn't believe our fortune. The two-plus years there at Bud's Shamrock Ranch were wonderful. After a while fellow pilots Tom "Elko" Ellison and Tom "Face" Riley joined us, and it goes without saying that Shamrock Ranch became the home of many festive events. When it would be a larger one, Bud would bring a whole pig and his big spit BBQer and roast the pig all day while we made other party preparations.

Other than the flying, the best part for me was the fact that I could ride my dirt bike—by then a two-stroke KTM 350, later a 500 (that I still have)—right out of the garage and into the desert and beyond. All of us at Shamrock, except "Face" (who drove a Jeep), had dirt bikes. At first we thought it was quite an achievement to ride out to Salt Wells (a brothel, never customers) on a salt flat just east of town, but in time we went much further. Steadily ranging further east, we eventually discovered Fredda Freeman's Middlegate bar, about fifty miles east, and became regular customers. On a weekend morning, we'd ride up and across the Stillwater Range to get there, have a few beers and a "Fredda burger," then ride back on a southern track that took us across Fairview Peak and the Fallon bombing range. On more than one occasion, we made our way back in the dark using flashlights and, on one of those trips, in blizzard conditions.

While in Fallon we also did three extended trips—two to Austin and the last to Eureka. Other squadron personnel got involved hauling the supplies and gas. While these took roads to our next camp spot or final destination, several of us on bikes would make our way across salt flats, sage-covered valleys, and pinon-pine-adorned mountains that rose three or four thousand feet above the valley floors. My sister, Katherine, and her dear friend Susan Hardy (nee Heon), both naval officers, came on the Austin trips and helped with the logistics and cooking. Around the campfire one night I, with my guitar, spontaneously composed a song for Katherine called "The Ripples in her Eyes," which touched her deeply. Even today she remembers the sweet song well—and rolls her eyes. Fredda had a sister in Austin who ran a saloon called the Owl Club, so on both of these adventures to Austin, we ended up celebrating there till the wee hours while a band from the local Indian reservation played the latest hits. On the way to Austin the first time, we visited one Mr.

Leo Kelly who had an old cabin at the middle of Gabbs dry lake. He mined something there, I don't recall what, and also there was a very nice hot spring. On that Austin trip, as well as a couple times before, we brought him Oreo cookies and batteries from town, and he let us enjoy his hot spring as long as we liked.

Now back to serving with the Cylons. I first learned to fly the Northrup F-5E Tiger and not long after re-learned to fly the Douglas A-4 Skyhawk. Our mission was "Navy Adversary." Our task was to play the mock role of enemy fighters in order to train Navy fighter pilots and air wings in general how to counter enemy airborne threats. Here, I was officially designated a fighter pilot, although what we flew was nowhere as hot or capable as the fleet fighter jets. Nevertheless, when, for example, the F/A-18 Hornet training squadron would come up from Lemoore with their fledgling fighter pilots, it was easy during the first few training flights to outmaneuver them. It didn't take long, however, for them to wise up and outmaneuver us with their superior machines.

The qualification to perform the "Adversary" mission was achieved by first learning to fly the aircraft just mentioned and then participating for two weeks with a Top Gun class at NAS Miramar. I was part of the Top Gun class but flew on the side of the Top Gun instructors. Because of my Light Attack background, and because I flew an old F-5E with a weak and obsolete radar the whole time, I got shot down many times and don't recall shooting anyone. On most of these missions, there were many aircraft in the air, and in the debriefs it used to amaze me how some of the pilots could remember all that happened. A few of them—not all instructors—would be able to describe what the other five or six aircraft were doing during the whole fight and replicate it on the white board. Then, it all looked like spaghetti to me. Nevertheless, I got through with a *laurel and hearty handshake* and went back to Fallon to do a watered-down version of what the Top Gun instructors did.

The just-mentioned Hornet training squadron would come up every month or so from Lemoore in order to train their students in the fine art of air-to-air warfare. Now it just so happened that my old pal Rico got a job there just about the time I came to the Cylons, and once we both had our respective qualifications, we met in Fallon on quite a few occasions. We'd brief, fly, debrief (sometimes do it again in a day), and maybe get together in the evening. His delightful wife, Mitzie, came up too a couple times, and we, along with a friend of theirs, overnighted at the old mining town of Virginia City. On another occasion they drove out to Middlegate while I rode my bike there, and we dined on Fredda burgers. During this time I learned a little more about his Christian faith and, without telling him, was quietly drawn to it. Sensing what a jam I'd be in if I stood guilty before God, I was tempted to accept it. At some point Rico gave me a small copy of C. S. Lewis's book *Mere Christianity*, but I didn't read it for quite some time. When I finally did, the circumstances were somewhat unusual, as I will now explain.

In February of 1990 I requested and was approved for a cross-country flight to the East Coast. The A-4F that the squadron provided was probably twenty years old by that time. A-4s had for two decades-plus been the Navy's main carrier-based Light Attack jet and were slowly replaced by the A-7 during and after the Vietnam War. For some reason I stuck Rico's book in my G-suit pocket when I left Shamrock Ranch that morning. The trip there involved a couple refueling stops and was uneventful. But on the way back in the middle of a huge winter storm, the shaft that goes from the engine to the CSD (constant speed drive) that then turns the main electrical generator sheered as I was flying at forty-two thousand feet over Minnesota. I was barely skimming the clouds, and the storm was everywhere under me. Battery power kicked in, but that could power things for only a few minutes, which was not near enough time to get me safely down through the clouds and to a safe landing. Without a powered and functioning attitude gyro (that tells the pilot up from down), there would be no hope. Fortunately, the A-4 had a little standby generator with a little propeller in front that could be flopped out into the wind stream, powered up, and used to provide power to vital aircraft components like the attitude gyro. This was accomplished by pulling vigorously on a handle that was like the handle used to start a lawn mower engine. In test flights I had found these RATs (ram air turbines) to be unreliable. Sometimes they worked, sometimes they didn't. If it didn't work now, I'd go out of control in the stormy clouds and have to eject (old A-4 ejection seats weren't exactly reliable either). So I took a deep breath (might have even lifted up a prayer) and pulled the handle, heard some whine on the headset, saw cockpit lights pulsate, then got signs that the RAT had indeed powered things successfully—at least for the moment. I breathed a sigh of relief but was far from out of the woods. I didn't know till later that the CSD shaft had sheered because of engine vibration caused by bad engine bearings. I was lucky that the engine kept running.

I then asked Minneapolis air traffic control where the nearest airport was that still had acceptable weather. He replied that Duluth was good for the moment, but snow would begin there soon. Hearing that, I headed north, descended through the clouds while sucking on my teeth (as Peewee would say), and landed at Duluth twenty minutes before it began to snow. In the next twenty-four hours it snowed two feet and got down to twenty-five degrees below zero. Being stuck there for a week in the bitter cold until a crew could get in and change the engine, I availed myself of the local ski hill, providentially called Spirit Mountain. Back at the cozy Duluth Air National Guard (ANG) base guest quarters, the Spirit of God worked on my heart as I read Rico's book. I don't remember the details, but I do recall thinking that what Lewis said was true and that I had no good reason not to submit myself to the authority of Christ.

When I got back to Fallon and weathered some complaining by the skipper regarding my and the plane's long absence, I spent some time over several evenings reading portions of the New Testament books of John and Romans. I also pondered the sinful things that I had done as well as the eternal price I would pay should I die unforgiven. God had spared me thus far but might not tomorrow.

One night shortly thereafter—I don't know why I didn't write down the exact date in my pocket pal calendar, but I know it was still February—I knelt next to my bed at Shamrock Ranch and told God that I had decided to believe in and submit myself to Jesus Christ, that I was sorry for my sins, and that I would do my best to do better in the future. There were no fireworks, just a simple decision. I slept pretty good that night.

Mom: AA Stewardess

Blessed Family

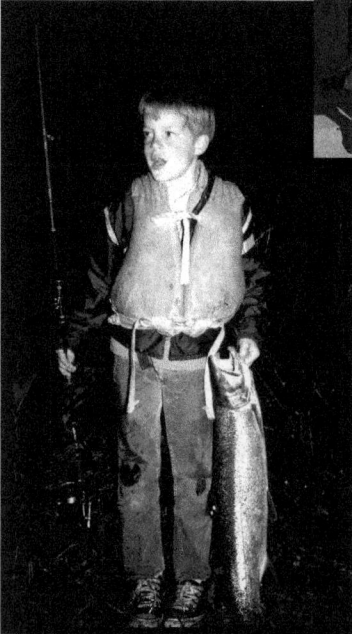

Big Steelhead

H Co. class of '82

Mary Kate Watkins

North American T-28 Trojan

A-7 training class at El Centro

A-7 cockpit: switch, knob, and dial Disneyland

VA-27 "Royal Maces" (aka "Chargers")

On the "foul line"

Chargers over the Vinson

Athena's farm

Somewhere over the Aleutians

Rico and Mitzi wedding in Thailand

Dan Anderson gutting a rattler

Virginia City Grand Prix finish

Cylon F-5 Tiger over central Nevada

Mom and Dad with harvest

Tom and Glenda Lovrich

Dr. Richard and Donna Rigsby

Dr. Patrick Todjeras

*Mark and
Irina Werth*

*The Blue
Danube*

*Success in Wien
(Dr. Loader
on rt.)*

"Friendly Bob" Miller

Moriahhof

Nick and Donna Geiger

Pastor Randy and Sandy Burk

"blessed is the man . . ."

PART TWO

Living for God

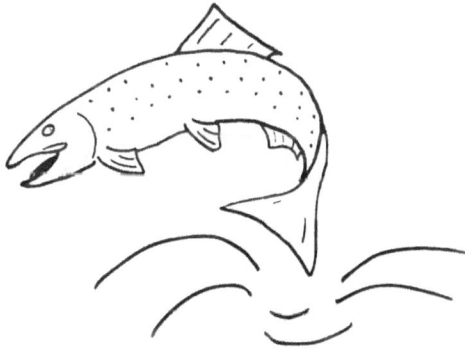

7

Fallon Follies and Navy Farewell

Flying with the Cylons continued apace, and it wasn't long till Rico came up again with a flock of fledgling fighter pilots to train. One evening we drove into town, and I mentioned to him, almost in an offhand way, that I had accepted Christ. His response—something like "that's great!"—was also casual. But unspoken, yet aware to both of us, was the enormous fact that I had made the most important decision that a man can ever make in his life.

That summer I was sent around the Pacific Fleet to evaluate squadrons and pilots that were still flying the venerable A-4. Besides other places closer to home, this included trips to the Philippines and Hawaii. While at the former, I did one or two things that I knew to be displeasing to God and then in Hawaii almost "bought the farm" when, in a two-seat A-4, the fellow I was evaluating came down so hard on a simulated emergency landing that the main brace on one of the main landing gear completely sheered. It was a bona fide miracle that the gear didn't collapse, which would have meant certain death for both of us. The Bible speaks much about the salvation that is available through faith in Christ. It also warns us about how unrepentant sinners—for example, thieves, swindlers, idolaters, drunkards, and the sexually immoral—will not "inherit the kingdom of God" (1 Corinthians 6:9-10). Perhaps, despite my recent profession of faith, if the gear had collapsed that day I would have nevertheless stood condemned.

Besides flying, my next love continued to be riding my bike. While still flying A-7s and on a detachment to Fallon, I saw a truck with a dirt bike in the bed and found out whose it was: LT Dan Anderson, who flew A-6s with another air wing. I found him, and we became good friends. For several years we had many fine adventures on our off-road machines. Several times I met him and his immediate and extended family—including his mom and dad—at the yearly family campout at the old ghost town of Masonic (a few miles from where the Bridgeport fire department almost brought me down that day). Only problem was that just about every time we rendezvoused, someone got injured.

On one of the family Masonic campouts, Dan and his brothers and I roared off on the first morning, and by noon one brother had a broken arm and Dan had a broken wrist. The brother threw in the towel for the weekend, but Dan moved the twist throttle on his bike from one handlebar side to the other and blasted off again with one arm in a sling. On another occasion Dan's brothers were badly shook up when they flipped their pickup with bikes in the bed, and then a little later while trying to load one of the bikes I accidentally yanked the entire middle fingernail out and broke the fingertip. Yet another time Dan came close to serious injury or death when he forgot on takeoff to put the flaps down on his homemade bush airplane, and later on the same excursion my arm was badly burned when I stupidly opened a boiling radiator.

Dan and I, along with his brother Eric, also raced the Virginia City Grand Prix in '89 and '90. The first time was a cold, rainy, snowy, and muddy mess, but I did a little better than Dan despite brake fluid continually boiling off. The next year Dan was ready and, in better conditions overall, bested me. Both years there were about five hundred racers. The first year I came in 111th place. The next year I came in 111th place. What were the chances?. We were going to do it again in '91 to get a best two out of three, and another 111th place for me, but I crashed while pre-running the course and was put out of commission.

These were some excellent times, but when in the course of these adventures I came to Christ, this came into some friction with the Mormon beliefs of Dan and his family. But they were always very gracious, and their mom was an expert at nursing the sick and wounded.

Because of my free-spirit nature and because of how I had seen the protective and merciful hand of God in the past, I tended from the start of my Christian life to be somewhat mystical. I desired signs from God. This tendency would in general move me further along but sometimes result in one or two wild goose chases. As the story proceeds from here, this tendency will be a recurring theme, and it began right away after my decision.

In the summer of 1990 I took a jet down to the Van Nuys, CA, airshow for the second time. Because of the confined airspace, there was no military flying during the show except for me—and only a fly-out on Sunday afternoon so I could get back to Fallon before closing. By the way, the Cylons had also made me coffee mess officer (my reputation proceeded me), and I had expanded the squadron offerings such that we made good money at airshows all over the nation. One of the top sellers was a poster with yours truly sitting in a dark cockpit with a laser beam coming out of his eye. That one had been the idea of our FedEx delivery driver, Mr. Geary Gard, a good Christian man who set up the photoshoot and produced the finished product. At airshows we'd sign the posters with big silver ink pens, and the locals would buy 'em up like hotcakes.

Anyways, at the end of the Van Nuys show, I got in the cockpit of my F-5 Tiger to fly out while ten thousand or so people watched intently. But all of a sudden I received a call from nature that couldn't be ignored and sheepishly climbed back out of the machine and made my way through the crowd toward the porta potties. They got a good laugh out of this. Just as I approached one of the open potties, I heard to my left, "Hey, Eric, we really enjoyed having you. Come back next year!" It was the airshow promoter's wife, a super friendly gal. So I walked over to her to say "thank you" and "see you next time," but as I did, she motioned to her left and said, "This is

Jackie," and introduced me to a pretty young lady working an ice cream stand. When I looked at her, it was as if the heavens parted and the angels sang. Some kind of supernatural impression came on me, and as I said, "How do you do," I immediately took it as some kind of romantic signaling from God. Then I quickly did my business in the porta potty, returned once more to the ladies, and slipped my business card to Jackie as I shook her hand one last time and said farewell. I then made my way back to the jet, with many still snickering, mounted up and blasted off in a blaze of afterburner glory—with Jackie glancing between the fighter rocketing above her head and the card in her hand.

Was it from God? I don't know for sure. Like much else of this genre, it worked out, but not in the way I expected. Some weeks later I received a letter from Jackie, and not long after that I met her in Los Angeles. We had a good time, but like with times before and after, the more I was romantically interested in a girl, the less inner peace I had. This has been such a rule that by and by I came to accept it in later years as God's *provision* so I would progress on in my life with Christ *alone*. I was at first romantically drawn, but after some pondering, I came to perceive that God used Jackie to introduce me to the place where she had gone to college and the place where I would a few years later go to seminary, that is, Biola University.

Then in Fallon I met a beautiful and charming lady named Carol, and once again some mystical notions took hold of me. Before I knew it, I had declared my love and offered to marry her. She agreed, and that summer and fall we had some good times together. At the same time, however, an inner force was driving me toward the future and meaningful things that seemed to transcend marriage. So only a few months later, I called off the engagement. I've never been married, and that was the only time I was engaged. One interesting aspect of this was the following: We were introduced by a woman who styled herself a white-witch of sorts and who confirmed the rightness of our relationship by a reading of Tarot cards. When we broke up, this woman exhibited a fierce anger that seemed to me at the time to be from the dark side.

Around this time I met a fellow fifteen years my senior who became a pretty good friend and fellow explorer of the Great Basin.

One early December day the squadron boys and their ladies were out in the mountains east of Fallon having fun in the snow and hunting down Christmas trees. While there, an old Chevy van went by and backfired. Later that day at Middlegate, Fredda introduced me to a man named Zeke (Mr. Wendall White). He asked, "How'd ya like the backfire?" He'd seen us just off the road and purposefully gave us the loud bang. Right off I could tell this was an interesting person. Over a beer or two he told me his story. He was a retired Sacramento area electrician (kids all grown by then) who spent as much time as possible riding dirt bikes and camping with friends in Nevada. Fredda had known him for a long time. Well, one thing led to another, and Zeke and I ended up having some supreme adventures together. Few ranchers knew the valleys and mountains of central Nevada better than he.

Our best adventure was a ride from the Shamrock Ranch to Eureka, NV, about four hundred miles along primitive trails that I had scouted out from the air. Several NAS friends, including Shamrock housemate Tom "Face" Riley, provided support, my nephew Dan (who'd been on the Tiger Cruise) took care of fuel logistics, and Carol managed the food and drink. Out of Middlegate, Zeke, along with his friend Mr. Kim Proctor, took me up to the high country of the Desatoya Range and showed me a WWII-era bomber wreck. Fredda and her new husband, Russ, rendezvoused with us later in the day. They had met not long before at a Boxcar Willie concert in Winnemucca and soon thereafter got married at a lovely mountain spot just east of Middlegate. We arranged for a Cylon F-5 to fly close by right when they said "I do."

On that first evening of the Eureka ride, Fredda fed everyone from a big kettle of chili that she and Russ had pre-prepared. The next day we went up and over the Shoshone, Toyabe, and Toquima ranges and camped out on a creek at the base of the Monitor Range that was loaded with rainbow trout. After catching some of those, Zeke and I took off on the bikes and for the next solid hour went as fast as we could, handlebar to handlebar, through the south end of the Monitor Range in a ballet that was absolutely perfect. By that time, I was riding a KTM 500, and Zeke had his Kawasaki 500, both two-strokes and crazy fast.

Upon return at dusk, we had our fill of trout and Carol's delicious fixin's, and a bit later we had to wear sunglasses after Zeke placed a VW engine block (made of magnesium) in the campfire. The whole valley shone like the sun! The next day the bikes went up through the Hot Creek Range and, after rendezvousing with the support trucks again, headed up Little Fish Lake Valley to Eureka where we had a good time at a saloon owned by yet another sister of Fredda. Both Zeke and I to this day remember this as being the zenith of our off-road adventures.

We also entered a desert race, the "Fallon to Lovelock 100," not long before I left Fallon. After a parade ride through town, they cut us and the other four hundred or so riders loose. From the start I lost track of Zeke and didn't see him till the finish line in Lovelock much later. About halfway through the race, I lost some time when I gave a broke-down rider a ride to the next checkpoint. That completed, I rocketed on ahead and finally, very tired, crossed the finish line a couple hours later. That evening at the post-race party we got the results. Zeke came in 93rd place, and I came in 94th. What were the chances of that?!

My ongoing romance with dirt bikes, and my adventurous spirit in general, probably didn't help me professionally in the Navy. All along, I was a good aviator and only a so-so officer, but the latter is mainly what determines ranking and promotion. Nevertheless I tried to stay in the Navy and actually got verbal orders to fly Hornets with the Golden Dragons who were forward deployed aboard the USS Independence in Japan. (Dream come true! Fighters on the "Indi" had recently replaced the Midway.) But I had to be promoted to O-4 (lieutenant commander) first. The word came one morning that the new LCDR list had been posted on the base of the Fallon control tower. So I drove there and read through the list. No "E. E. Engleman." I started at the top of the list again and went to the bottom. My name was not there. Man, was I totally bummed out but really not that surprised. Providing some headwinds in this regard was also the fact that Desert Storm had just ended, and the Navy was looking to cull their officer ranks somewhat. So I went to the squadron, sheepishly told my mates the results, and moped around for the next week or so.

But mulling things over, this was somewhat of a relief in that I no longer had to fret about how I would get by in the Navy with even more responsibility and officer duties to do. Plus, since I was a kid, I had also daydreamed about flying big airliners for some great airline company. I had lots of pilot-in-command time back then flying my little plastic model Japan Air Lines DC-8 all around the chicken yard, and now I would have the chance to do the real thing! I also, by that time, was feeling that perhaps God had more meaningful things for me to do for Him, and that could be somewhere other than the Navy. With all this under consideration, I made the decision to "be happy" and make my last several months in the Navy the best yet. So that's what I did, and, indeed, those last days were wonderful.

A bit later, I was directed to go down to Mexico City and help teach the Mexican Air Force fighter tactics. Then, the Mexicans had only one fighter squadron (flying Northrop F-5s). They knew how to bomb and strafe but had not yet learned the art of air-to-air combat (a restriction, as I recall, imposed upon them by the Mexican government). Once there I first spent several airborne sessions re-qualifying the US Air Force exchange pilot assigned to the squadron in ACM (air combat maneuvering). "Pedro,"[4] who spoke fluent Spanish, had been with the Jaguars for some time but, having done no ACM with them, had become unqualified in that regime according to USAF standards. So I got him back up to snuff, then together we trained up the CO of the squadron in the air-to-air martial art. To do that we really had to start with the basics, but the CO progressed quickly.

From the beginning the Jaguars had been brought up on USAF ways of doing things. Thus things were far more standardized than what I was used to. Very generally speaking, the Air Force then had the overarching principle, "Unless something is permitted, it is prohibited." The Navy was opposite: "Unless something is prohibited, it is permitted." I suppose this Navy ethos developed over centuries and many wars due to tradition and the unique and vast variety of circumstances that are possible when ranging all over the world dealing with countless unpredictable conditions. In other words, every circumstance cannot be foreseen and *permitted*. Local

---

4. Call sign.

commanders by necessity must make independent decisions. I'm glad I was a pilot in the Navy and not the Air Force.

While with the Jaguars, I got several great photos of Pedro over Aztec pyramids and the smoking volcano Popocatépetl. All in all it was a great time, but one night at a squadron dinner party the Jaguar boys got me quite drunk with the best tequila that the Aztecs could offer. I knew, however, that as a new Christian, this wasn't the best way to go.

Now just a few more short stories before I bring my Navy days to a close. One of my last duties with the Cylons was to go to MCAS (Marine Corps Air Station) El Toro, along with a few other pilots, and work with a class of their new fighter pilots. Toward the end of the week of the detachment I had a day off. Between meeting Jackie at the Van Nuys air show the year before and now, I had not forgotten that she was a graduate of Biola University in nearby La Mirada. So, moved by the Spirit, I drove up to this school, drove around it, watched a woman appear to preach to a tree, then went inside the admin building and spoke to someone who told me a little about the school. It was not only an undergrad university with about four thousand students, but it also possessed a seminary—Talbot School of Theology—that offered training for Christian pastors, missionaries, and scholars. When I left, I felt like God had nudged me regarding this place, but I kept it all to myself.

A few weeks later, Rico joined me in a two-seat A-4, and we flew up to Portland where we gave a presentation to the Portland Navy Club. Dad had actually arranged the event and beamed with pride as we showed slides and talked all about our experiences in naval aviation—including how God had worked in my life through Rico. One interesting guest we met there was the man who defected the USSR to Japan in a MiG-25 Foxbat fighter jet in 1976, LT Viktor Belenko. By that time he was a US citizen and quite a colorful person.

Finally, my old shipmate and band leader "Brick" Imerman brought up four A-7s from Lemoore and did battle with a couple of us Cylons over Gabbs dry lake just south of Fallon. Four lumbering Corsairs against two nimble F-5E Tigers piloted by very experienced Navy adversary pilots. We hit the merge smugly, and they creamed us! Every time I looked over my shoulder, there was Brick or one of his buddies on my tail saying, "Guns, guns, guns!" or "Fox 2!" (meaning "shot dead with a Sidewinder missile"). Our tails were firmly between our legs as we landed back in Fallon. This was the first of two pre-departure humblings.

The next came not long after (late January 1992) on my last flight in the Navy. It was a 2 v. 2, LCDR "Bear" Poulos and the "Bhagwan" against two fellow Shamrock Ranchers, "Boner" and "Elko." We hammered 'em pretty good on the first fight, and on the second round, Bear bagged Elko (or was it the other way around?), but I lost sight of Boner in a crafty vertical move and got gunned as a result. The old adage again proved true: "Lose sight, lose the fight." *But why,* I thought, *on my last flight!?* Thus I left my Navy career on a humbling note, which was probably, for me, a good thing.

Having another half hour or so of fuel left, I told the boys I'd see 'em back on deck and proceeded to cruise at low level alone across the valleys and mountains of my beloved Nevada, all the while with the surreal knowledge that this would be it. What a glorious time it had been. But something happened that had never happened before. Toward the end of that half hour, I actually got a little bit bored. So I headed back to base before expending all my fuel. It was time to go home. Been there, done that. Time to close the book and open another. While taxiing in, the base fire truck shot a stream of water over the plane—an ancient tradition—and when I exited the cockpit, the ground crew doused me with a big bucket of water. Through it all, God had been very, very good to me.

8

Riding Sidesaddle with AA: The Pruning Begins!

D ear reader, the adventure that I will describe in the remaining portion of the book will be, for some, not quite as exciting as what we've seen so far; however, it will nonetheless be an adventure in that God in my post-Navy life has repeatedly done "far more abundantly beyond all that [I could] ask or think, according to the power" that only He can bestow (Ephesians 3:20). From here on, I'll go at a quicker pace and hope to bless you with some remarkable stories of God's guidance and provision. Some may even find what follows to be more of a blessing than what preceded.

VFA-127 gave me a hearty farewell party and a photo album with many squadron memories, and I was sent off officially in fine style by Skipper CDR Vance "Steamer" Toalson. Also about that time Rico and Peewee and Brick arranged a farewell party for me at a rustic and run-down marina bar back in Lemoore. Brick got parts of the Light Attack All-Star band back together, and we played the night away while many friends from earlier days had a good time. There, Rico presented to me an award prepared by Peewee for my performance in a Cylon dogfighting tournament that had gone down a couple years before but for which I had not been properly recognized. That darn near brought me to tears. Then, as the party really started getting good, everyone was good 'n lubed, and the DJ was blasting the B-52s "Love Shack," a drunken sailor hit the power pole just outside the bar, and the transformer came crashing down and exploded. The cries of "Love shack babyyyy!" in an instant went silent, and the bar's owner started yelling for everyone to get out. It was as if the Lord was saying, *Eric, thank you for your service—but it's now OVER!* So, that was it. My unofficial final act in the US Navy. I will always love Rico and Peewee and Brick for doing what they did to make my finale special.

After saying goodbye to my squadron mates and ranch mates in Fallon, I drove north and spent a few months with Mom and Dad. This time I was busy applying to the airlines and doing what it took to ensure success with that. Right away, two major airlines were out. I should have earned here the call sign awarded to a fellow Fallon aviator who accidentally shot himself in the foot with a pistol: "DASH" (dumb $*& shot himself). After sending Delta and Continental Airlines applications, Delta wrote back and said, "Thank you, but we are not accepting Continental applications at this time." And Continental wrote back and said, "Thank you, but we are not accepting Delta applications at this time," or words to that effect. But, happily, I sent the right application to American, and, after a couple of lengthy interviews, they hired me. When I got the good news over the phone at the ranch, I gave a thumbs up to Mom and Dad, and they grabbed each other and danced joyfully around the kitchen. It was especially special because, as might be recalled, Mom had worked for AA and Mom had met Dad on an AA flight.

In early June 1992 I headed east to commence training with American. On the way there, I climbed Wheeler Peak in eastern Nevada (the same peak that Rhino and I had skimmed over six years before). Then, passing through Aspen, CO, I got the hair-brained idea of climbing Colorado's highest mountain—Mt. Elbert, 14,440 feet—at night under a full moon. After consulting a map or two, I figured I could ride my bike up an old mining road to about eleven thousand feet and from there go on foot straight up the northwestern slope. The eastern side of the mountain had a trail to the top, but there was none on this side.

The first phase went according to plan. At dusk, I unloaded my KTM at a small campground and rode three or so miles up the Arkansas River, which was high with spring glacial runoff. Then I crossed the river on a narrow footbridge and headed up a rough trail several miles and parked at the base of the mountain just before the trail ended at an abandoned mine. The way up was not too bad, just going from boulder to boulder on a pretty steep incline up about three thousand feet. Even though the moon was then on the other side of the mountain, I wondered why, on a cloudless night, there wasn't more light. With about five hundred feet to go, I had to cross a snowfield near a deep ravine, but the wind, which had increased the higher I got, pushed me toward the ravine despite my efforts to keep going up. So I decided it best to abort the mission at that point. About then, the moon finally rose over the summit above, and I discovered why everything was still so dark: the moon was eclipsed! Not a good omen. So I hunkered down in a cleft in the rock, ate a PB&J sandwich, prayed, and began the descent—very carefully. It was then about midnight.

At about 3 a.m. I arrived at the bike. It had been blown over by the wind, but, in my slightly hypoxic state, I wondered if a big grizzly bear had done it. After strapping my mini Maglite to the front fender, I fired the bike up and headed down the canyon. When I approached the river crossing again, there was a big tree that I had not previously noticed just short of the beginning of the footbridge. Unlike earlier, I couldn't get a run at the narrow bridge and, because of that, lost my balance once I started the crossing. To correct, I put out my right foot, but it only met thin air. So over I went into the freezing river where I ended up on the bottom with the bike on top of me. Right at that moment I was impressed by the absurdity of the situation and, of course, the bitterly cold water.

With all my strength I was able to push the bike off and get my head above water. God gave me that strength. The mini Maglite was still doing its job, the faint light shining on the rocky river bottom. Then, using the strong current, I was able to use the bike like a sail and slowly get to the far side where I wrestled the heavy machine up and out of the river. Once on the northern bank, it took about an hour to get the water and debris and trout out of the air box, carburetor, and engine. The trusty machine then started after a few kicks, and I rode back to camp where I made a fire, warmed up, then went to bed just as the sun was coming up.

A day or two later, and a day before commencing training with American, as I was rolling down the road in "Bob" across the New Mexico border into Texas, I thought long and hard about my drinking and partying past. Because of that, there had been stupidity, damage, and poor treatment of women, and I'd even flown hungover a time or two. But now I knew that the Bible condemned drunkenness, and I would now have a hundred-plus people on the airplane relying on me to transport them safely.

The other hard decision to end all sexual immorality had been decided before I left Fallon. But I had put off this one because alcohol had been such an ongoing and highly desired part of my life. While under the influence, it had made me braver, happier, and more sociable, but also stupider and more likely to sin. It had been a miracle that I had never gotten a DUI or crashed while drunk. Fornication and boozing were two things I really did not want to give up, but I now knew that if I were to really be a "friend" of Jesus and really be a better man, I had to first obey Him and get past these two serious sins. The former already being put away, there passing through the barren lands of west Texas I made a firm decision to also put away the latter. That was a very difficult decision that took many miles cruising down the highway to make. It was an agonizing ordeal, but I finally submitted to the Spirit. I have stuck to this decision through the years, although now and again I have allowed a bit of moderation when it has come to social situations where the consumption of a small amount of alcohol allowed me to not unnecessarily offend my host. In any case, since that day, I've never been drunk or even close to it—by God's grace.

After all I'd been through in the Navy, I assumed that initial training with American would be a cakewalk. I was wrong. The pace of training in the Navy was brisk but not frantic; the pace of training at American was frantic-plus! I forgot to factor in that I was no longer a *public* servant but now a *private* servant where efficiency to maximize profits was the priority. Several of us in the initial Boeing 727 FE (flight engineer) training were assigned an instructor who had many years before piloted for Braniff Airlines and was definitely of the "old school" mentality. He would holler at us as we took turns dealing with all kinds of emergency situations in the simulator and slam his old-style wooden pointer close to our fingers if we reached for the wrong switch, button, or knob. There was so much to learn in such a short time, and all this had to be correctly applied in the many intense simulator sessions.

During these few months, I learned that, try as I might, my learning pace was below average. My roommate, Mark, a very friendly Air Force fighter pilot, would often be out till late, return and crack his books for an hour or so while watching TV, then be asleep by midnight. Meanwhile, I would study the entire evening and even after he went to sleep. Nevertheless, he excelled, and I fell behind. He was at the top of the class, and I got knocked behind a class or two because of failed simulator rides. Even those who had come from civilian backgrounds flying commuter and regional planes did better. And I was the hot-shot fighter pilot! Looking back, it seems that this was the Lord's beginning of the long process of my humble-ization—something the Bible calls *pruning*—that I would need massive doses of before I would be fit to effectively serve Him. By and by, I finally had success and was directed to report to the AA Flight Office at LaGuardia Airport in Queens, New York.

When I flew that little JAL DC-8 around the chicken yard as a kid, I was the big cheese, the pilot-in-command, the captain. But the problem now was that I was sitting sidesaddle running the plethora of electrical, fuel, pneumatic, and hydraulic systems, and captains and first officers (co-pilots) often younger than me were barking out orders. Those orders sometimes had to do with something I was doing wrong with the aircraft's systems and sometimes had to do with getting them coffee or scrounging up meals or cookies from the flight attendants. More humble-ization! The FE job then didn't pay well, was often boring, and was frankly beneath the dignity of a seasoned Navy attack/fighter aviator. Nevertheless, I was thrilled to finally be an *airline pilot*! Overall, it was a good job—grousing aside—and I tried to make the most of it.

Continuing to feel the call to serve Christ, I began attending a small Dutch Reformed church in Kew Gardens (a part of Queens). They didn't have much in the way of music going on, so I formed a little worship band that first consisted of me singing and playing guitar with a couple fellows on base and drums. Before this I had never served any church.

About that time I had the worst FE flight of my FE career. The captain was an older no-nonsense fellow who took umbrage at what he saw as my cavalier attitude, but I didn't perceive it at first. Toward the end of the second day, he got so mad that he looked like the Enterprise air boss who wanted to strangle me years before, with veins bulging but this time with a fist pulled back. I honestly did not try to provoke him, and I told him so. On the last day of the sequence he calmed down some, but by the time I got back to Operations at LaGuardia, I really felt crushed. So I slumped down in one of the couches there and fell asleep.

A little later, a noise woke me up, and there right next to me was an attractive F/A (flight attendant) trying to use the telephone right by my left arm. I introduced myself and we got to talking and discovered that we both lived in "crash pads" in the same apartment complex. Lisa would confess much later that she had engineered the telephone call in order to meet me. I was handsomer then. One thing led to another, and Lisa became my right-hand girl at the church, playing the piano in the worship band. She was a good friend my entire time there in Queens, and we shared many a slice of cheese pie and many a bowl of matzo ball soup. A little later, another American F/A whom I'd met, Joyce, joined the worship band with her wonderful voice, and then we really had a quality thing going.

Speaking of music and ticked-off captains, I got in a bit of hot water one evening while cruising to (maybe it was from) Nashville when I played a few bars of "Oh Suzanna" on my harmonica for Mrs. Dolly Parton who was sitting just behind the cockpit. She responded graciously with, "You'll have to come and play with my band!" But the captain was not happy that I'd done it, perceiving a bit of dereliction of duty in my impromptu performance. I suppose he was right.

After I'd been in Queens for more than a year (October of '93), several of us from the church headed out on a chilly morning for a day-long retreat at a Christian facility about fifty miles north near the Hudson River. For some time I had been badgering Mark Sanchez, the pastor, about my need to be baptized, but he kept putting it off. On the way to the retreat, I saw a creek through the yellow and orange leaves of the autumn trees and exclaimed to Mark, "Hey, there's a creek big enough to baptize!" So we stopped, and Mark and I slid down about a hundred feet of slippery slope, and there he dunked me completely under the cold water "in the name of the Father, the Son, and the Holy Spirit." The rest of the crew still up by the van clapped with joy and approval as I came up out of the water.

The flying out of NYC with American was a pleasure overall and a blessing, but deep down I felt that the Lord had greater things for me in store. So I prayed much about it. I would have been happier at American if I had marched up the seniority ladder quickly, but as fate had it, I was hired at the end of a long hiring boom, and now I was stuck at the bottom rung of the ladder as an FE with no first officer let alone captain promotion in sight. Actually, American started laying off pilots about the time I was baptized, and I figured that I'd better come up with an alternate plan in case they got to me. Among other possibilities, I looked into serving God as a missionary aviator flying people and supplies in and out of exotic far-away places. Looking further into that, I visited JAARS (Jungle Aviation and Relay Service), a Christian mission aviation outfit in Waxhaw, NC, and learned a little about their work. With them, as with a similar outfit I talked to, there didn't seem to be so much of a need for pilots as for other occupations, and in any case, the pilots spent most of their time doing management tasks anyways. My JAARS hosts were hospitable, but in general their interest in me seemed somewhat lukewarm.

At the end of the day in Waxhaw, they thanked me for coming and invited me before leaving to take their nature walk just beside the office building. So I did that, and it was quite lovely. At the end of the walk there was a strange-looking box set on a stand at waist level. Written on the box was something like this:

Push this button to hear a message from JAARS' founder, Mr. Cameron Townsend.

I pushed the button, and in an obviously very old and scratchy recording, Mr. Townsend gave a message about the great value of Christian missions. His last words were what caught my attention. They went something like this: "Thank you for listening so politely to my message about the importance of missions. It has been a pleasure to speak with you here today at Biola College." This immediately brought back the memory of Jackie at the Van Nuys airshow and my subsequent visit to Biola where I perceived the Spirit whispering. As I left Waxhaw that day and flew back to New York, I felt like the Lord had again whispered.

A little later I saw Pastor Charles Stanley on the TV, and he said, "If you think that God is telling you to do something, and you've prayed about it and sought counsel concerning it, and still haven't done it, then step out in faith and do it!" At the moment he said "step out," Stanley stepped off the stage, and because I couldn't see what was below his feet, I assumed he was going to tumble down into the crowd. But there was a step there that was just out of the picture, so all was fine. That "step out" just as he stepped out really impressed me, so I said to myself, *OK, I'll do it!* A few days later, I put in a request for a leave of absence to get a jump on things. I knew I was going to get laid off anyways. This was approved, and mid-summer of 1994 I said goodbye to the church and to Lisa and headed again toward California.

9

Westward Ho!
to the Bible Institute
of the Angels

On the way west, a trivial incident was emblematic of how God has dealt with me all along. Passing through Ohio, one of the front tires suddenly went flat as I stopped at a stop sign. So I looked to my left—only corn fields—then looked to my right, Goodyear Tire Center. There was also a sign there: "Welcome to Akron!"

In Salt Lake City, I picked up our old family friend Bob Young (with whom I had provoked Mt. St. Helens long before). I had met Bob and his lovely wife, Sud, the previous summer in Colorado where we backpacked a bit, fished, and successfully climbed Mt. Elbert via the same route that I had attempted the year before. Our plan this time was to head west and climb a couple of peaks, the first being Mt. Moriah right on the Utah/Nevada border, and then Mt. Morey in central Nevada. As we proceeded to within sight of the first mountain, Bob was asleep, and I found myself in no mood to start a rigorous multi-day climb. So as a solo decision, I decided to bypass Moriah and perhaps simply stay the night at a comfy motel in Ely.

Right at that moment, I saw a gravel road off to the right and a sign that read, "To Eskdale," and suddenly I remembered a car at

CONFESSIONS OF A CUTTHROAT TROUT

that very intersection two years before (as I headed east to start with AA) with Amish-like people in it. It seemed supernatural that such a thing would come back to mind two years later. I involuntarily said something like, "Huh!" and that woke Bob up. He said, "What's up?" and I told him what had just happened. So he said, "Let's go take a look." I turned around, went back to the intersection, and went down a long dirt road to Eskdale (and eventually to Mt. Moriah).

Turned out that the little village was a self-sufficient, religious society of men, women, and children founded some forty years before by one Mr. Maurice Glendenning. The current leader of the commune, Dr. Conrad, who had previously been a Mormon, gave us a tour then invited us into his office where he told us of the history and purpose of the community. The men believe that they are descendants of the first Israelite high priest, Aaron, and have decided to live in the remote Utah desert in order to prepare for the return of Christ and the reestablishment of His kingdom in Jerusalem. Then they will serve as priests in the millennial temple there. At the time, all this sounded a little bit strange, yet it seemed providential that we were there.

After a discussion about this, we thanked him for his hospitality then went to get into my truck, but one of the tires was flat (again!). One of the fellows who walked us out said, "No problem, just pull into the drive-through garage over there, and we'll fix it." So that's what we did, and as they got to work with wives and their toddlers looking on, we mentioned our original intent to climb Mt. Moriah— which could be seen out the far side of the garage. They told us how to get there and what a beautiful place it is. Tire finally repaired, we thanked them and headed toward Moriah.

Reflecting on all this, it seemed to me that God wanted us to go up Mt. Moriah after all and that He brought that about through men who considered themselves to be descendants of Aaron and, long before him, Abraham who took his son Isaac to "the mountains of Moriah" to offer him up as a sacrifice—as per God's direction (see Genesis 22). In other words, because of laziness I was going to pass up Moriah, but men who believe that they will one day be priests serving atop the Jewish Moriah providentially redirected us to the top of the Nevada Moriah. Little did I know then that by year's end, I would also stand atop the Jewish Moriah in Jerusalem!

The climb up Mt. Moriah—elevation 12,072 feet—was quite arduous. From trailhead to summit was about five thousand feet of elevation gain and eight miles, so we had to camp part way up. The final push to the top was trail-less and steep. The view from the summit was worth the effort. We could see a hundred miles-plus in every direction and were all alone. About three-fourths the way up, there was a large spring that came right out of the side of the mountain. Later I would dream about this spring in a special way.

After Moriah we went to even more remote country in Nevada, camped (at a spot that I had passed by three years previous on the Eureka ride), and the next day ascended Mt. Morey of the Hot Creek Range (10,240 feet). The terrain near the top really got steep, and Bob with his bad eyes struggled some, but we finally made it. There was a climbing register at the top (just a rusty tin can with a ratty notebook inside). The last party to climb the peak were Sierra clubbers a year previous. The mountain was very lonely. Yet the BLM and Forest Service, at the insistence of the Sierra Club and other environmentalists, were then in the process of protecting the place from people. New signs surrounded the remote mountain warning, "Wilderness!" which meant for most, "Keep Out!" The Sierra Club, and other earth worshippers, wanted it all for themselves.

We then headed for Reno so Bob could fly back home. On the way there, we visited Fredda and Russ at Middlegate. She asked why I never returned to get my household stuff that I had stored there. Frankly, I had completely forgotten about it but told her I'd pick it up soon. But she said not to worry about it because the storage building and all my stuff had burned down. Easy come, easy go! I then left (my friend) Bob off in Reno and picked up my sister Ginny's husband, Phil, and we headed out a little east of Middlegate for some camping and fossil hunting. Phil, an engineer and liked by all, was skeptical regarding religious claims and considered fossils to be evidence of the evolutionary scheme. I tried to account for them, on the other hand, by God's supernatural creation and the flood in Noah's day that killed all life—save the humans and animals on the ark. Evolution says that life on earth has been growing more complex and orderly. But this is hard to square with a universe that generally tends toward decay and disorganization. I probably pushed a little too hard on that trip. But we found lots of fish and plant fossils and had a good time.

After dropping Phil off in Reno, I went back out to Middlegate and met my old friend Dan Anderson and his family, as well as Zeke and a friend of his, for what I hoped to be a memorable multi-day, off-road adventure. In my spirit, though, I felt a little bit like this was a step backward. There at Fredda's, I laid a map out on the pool table with the proposed route. We'd be progressing east every day and camping at a different spot each night. The Andersons resisted, however, thinking that riding out of a base camp would be better overall, especially since their mother was along for the trip too. But I selfishly insisted, wanting to explore yet-uncharted territory, so we pressed on. This time, Dan would not ride but fly in his homemade bush airplane and help scout the route from the air while he stayed in radio contact via walkie-talkie.

Dan's near crash when he forgot to put his flaps down for takeoff from Fredda's parking lot set the tone for the rest of the trip. A little later Eric (Dan's brother) started having trouble with his old Husqvarna bike and finally came to a stop. I stupidly removed the radiator cap before it had cooled down and burned my entire forearm badly. In a lot of pain, I had to tow him with my bike for about five miles to where we could rendezvous with Dan as well as his mom who was in a support car. After his mom covered my arm with aloe vera and stuck it in a cooler of ice, I gave my KTM to Eric to ride, and I continued on with Dan in his Kitfox daredevil machine—quite crestfallen. Late in the day, as Eric was going full bore up a long valley, a cooling line broke, but he didn't know it, and the engine overheated and seized. By and by we all arrived alive at the first camp, but, given all the problems, we decided to stay there for the remainder of our adventure. At least we were all alive, but both my bike as well as Eric's were down for the count.

During the next couple days, much of the time was spent around the campfire debating Christianity vs. Mormonism, mainly regarding the faith vs. works issue. I did my best to put the emphasis on the Apostle Paul's words: "By grace you have been saved through faith; and that not of yourselves, it is the gift of God" (Ephesians 2:8). On the last day my arm felt calmed down enough to venture a ride. So Eric and I borrowed bikes and went up and across the Desatoya Range and found Zeke and his friend having a beer at Cold Springs (just northeast of Middlegate). They had gotten tired of the religious debate and gone their own way.

Despite the arm pain, the ride back to camp was a blast, and I thus developed a better friendship with Eric. When I said goodbye to all the next morning and drove away, I started crying because what I expected to be a great time turned out to be a lot of pain and stress and arguing. It seemed that God was moving me away from this Mormon family who had been so good to me. Only then was I beginning to understand these words of Christ: "You follow Me!"

After a blessed visit with my father and mother in Washougal, I at last arrived in Los Angeles to begin Christian training at Talbot School of Theology, which is the seminary department of Biola University. Looking back at it now, it seems that I must have been quite naïve and immodest to think I should begin training as a pastor so soon after conversion and so soon after leaving major sins behind. The worst sin still substantially remained—*pride*. I was largely ignorant of the Bible and still full of uncleanness in my soul. Did God really tell me to "go"? I don't know for sure, but I was convinced at the time that He did, and even though there has been many ups and downs since then, I still think that God was in it.

The night before arriving there, I drove up in the local San Gabriel Mountains, found a trail, put a sleeping bag on my back, and ended up staying the night just short of the summit of San Gabriel Peak (6,164 feet). When the sun came up, I went on to the top, and there I prayed about the coming time at Talbot. Then it occurred to me that the "angel man" (*Engleman* in German) was on top of the arch-angel's (Gabriel's) peak in the arch-angel's mountain range, looking down at "the city of the angels" (Los Angeles) where I would soon attend the seminary at the "Bible Institute of the Angels" (*Bible Institute of Los Angeles*, the original name of the school, and the acronym basis for Biola)—all this while praying to the God who made the angels and whose one and only Son is the holy "angel of the covenant" (Malachi 3:1). Angels everywhere! Thus I got off to a very angelic start, and it seemed like confirmation that I was doing the right thing.

During the first year at Talbot ('94–'95) I lived in an old coed dorm on campus and quickly made friends. The campus oozed Christian spirit and purpose. But that first semester I found some of the classes to be quite hard. I didn't realize that Talbot was arguably the premier evangelical seminary in the Southwest from which many non-denominational churches (and denominational too), both small and big, derive their pastors. The master of divinity (MDiv) was more rigorous than most, and quite pricy too, but most importantly it was a very conservative and Spirit-filled program. The initial curriculum included New Testament Greek, Bible hermeneutics (interpretation), and the study of the church fathers (patristic theology). Right away, I hit the ground running in Greek and did very well. Bible hermeneutics was OK, but some of it baffled me. When I couldn't make hide nor hair of the very first patristic theology reading assignment, even after multiple attempts, I was reduced to tears that night with the thought, *Lord, You brought me here, but I don't understand a thing!* I took a break, prayed earnestly for understanding, and started reading again—and this time it started coming to me. Everything went tolerably well from there on.

One of my classmates about then saw that I had a dirt bike and told me that the Hebrew professor Dr. Richard Rigsby had a son who rode off road. A little later, Dr. Rigsby substituted in my hermeneutics class, so after it was over I went up to him, introduced myself, and asked him if his son rode dirt bikes. He said "yes" then slowly slipped his arm around me, looked me right in the eye, and intensely asked, "Have you ever been to Israel?" I learned right then that Dr. Rigsby and his delightful wife, Donna, had been the long-time leaders of the yearly Talbot Holy Land expeditions, and, little did I know, while I had dirt biking on my mind, Dr. Rigsby was using my query as an opportunity to recruit yet another "son" into their "Talbot Israel" family.

Not long thereafter, I decided to join them on the next trip— scheduled to depart just after Christmas that year. Nevertheless, Dr. Rigsby's son, John, and I did partner together on some excellent dirt bike adventures off and on during the next five years. Our goal was to find a way, off road, through the San Gabriel Mountains on over to the San Bernardino Mountains. We called it the "Burbank to Big Bear" mission. We actually were able to execute some large segments of it. But on one very hot day when we, terribly dehydrated and overheated, burst out of thick brush onto a live archery range with the owner yelling at us, John began having second thoughts about the mission's feasibility. Plus, on several occasions, we ran out of fuel while still a long way from base camp, which caused everyone to worry when we didn't show up till well after dark.

Early that first year I met a Biola student named Lilly.[5] Because of a few events I took as providential, I became convinced that she was "the one." Problem was, she perceived nothing of the sort and considered my attempts to get to know her something of a nuisance. Yet, I was quite sure that God had whispered to me about her. Later that year I learned that Dad was dying of cancer. By this time I had spoken to him quite a few times about my new faith. When first told about my conversion, he said, "That's fine, just don't be a fanatic." His somewhat arm's length relationship with Christ seemed to continue up till his final days. After the last day of class in the late Spring of 1995, I knelt next to my dorm bed in tears over these two situations and prayed earnestly for God to give salvation to my dad and clarity about Lilly. I stayed in that position for quite some time and for a moment (as I have often been prone to do when praying) dozed off. I'm convinced to this day that the Lord gave me a dream at that moment that He used to comfort me, but not necessarily say "yes" or "no." The dream consisted only of this: I was looking intently at myself in the eye, shaking my finger sternly, and saying, "Psalm 34:15, Psalm 34:15!" Then I woke up, finished praying, and got my Bible to see what Psalm 34:15 said, not being familiar with it at all: "The eyes of the LORD are toward the righteous, and His ears are open to their cry." Reading that comforted me greatly and amazed me at God's goodness and compassion. He heard me and would do what was best in His eyes, for "the LORD is righteous in all His ways and kind in all His deeds" (Psalm 145:17).

That summer while I was home, Dad died. But I was able to spend some quality time with him just before. This time we had some

5. Pseudonym

hallowed and, and on one or two occasions, humorous moments. Regarding the latter, a week or so before he died, I, in somewhat of a desperate spiritual frame of mind, prayed earnestly over him for God to eject any possible demons out of his body and soul so that he then might be free to freely choose Christ. Not that I had any evidence of demon influence at all, I just didn't know at that moment what else to do. I thought Dad was in a coma, but suddenly he opened his eyes, looked at me, and said, "Are you crazy?!"

A few days after that, Dad, with all of us gathered around him in the Vancouver hospital, gave us his final blessings. This was made possible somewhat because I pressured the hospice personnel to back off the heavy sedation. He said that he was leaving me a significant amount of money and that he wanted me to use it to complete my seminary education. That brought me to heavy tears, perceiving it as an indication of Dad's love and real spiritual state as well as an endorsement of my faith and theological training. And, as circumstances would have it, I was almost broke. Still, when he died a day or two later, not long before dawn, I was filled with dread when I was awakened and told.

That night, God again comforted me with a dream. In this one, I was deep inside the bowels of a ship in what seemed to be a horrible storm. In deep fear, I opened a porthole to get a glimpse of the raging sea, but when I looked out, the sea, to my surprise, was mostly smooth. Not far away was a naval ship weaving back and forth gaily with not a care in the world. As I marveled at this, the happy ship slowly receded astern of us and after some time disappeared over the horizon. But just before going out of sight, a Navy band came up topside and struck up a lively tune, then they and the ship were gone. Then I woke up, sure that God had spoken to me, and jotted down the contents of the dream lest I forgot them. But I couldn't remember the song that the band had played, and I felt like the song had much to do with the meaning of the dream. A little later, though, while in prayer, the song came to me: "When the Saints Go Marching In." With that, I believed that the good Lord had assured me that my father was one of the redeemed, and I praised Him for it. Did God *really* speak to me? I was convinced then, and I still believe it today. But I won't find out *for sure* till I'm in glory myself.

When school started up again, my good friend Bill March invited me to visit his church in Bellflower and consider serving there. Bill and I had gotten to know each other on the Talbot Israel trip at the first of the year. Dr. and Donna Rigsby led that trip, Mr. Gordon Franz—a theologian-archeologist from New Jersey—did most of the on-site lecturing, and we visited just about every notable site of the Bible the two weeks we were there. On one of the first days riding the bus, Bill heard me strumming Rush's "Fly by Night" on a guitar, which amazed him as he had been a Rush fan for years and had played, or rather drummed, their songs countless times. By my second Talbot year we were pretty good friends. As it turned out, I ended up serving at Bill's church—Bethel Grace Baptist Church—as his assistant in the youth ministry, and, best of all, I ended up living with his aunt and her husband when the next summer came around. Tom and Glenda Lovrich, who lived in a quaint house near the bay in Long Beach, had raised Bill in his teen years after his father and mother died. Now, Bill was about to get married, and his bunk would soon be available. So they invited me to stay over the summer break (1996). I ended up staying four glorious years while I pursued my master of divinity. Tom and Glenda were so gracious and hospitable and good to me. I will forever be thankful for the love they showed me and thankful that Bill loved his brother enough to make him part of his family.

Glenda was a first-class Christian and homemaker. Before being married, she had worked for some years at the Salvation Army station in east LA ministering to the urban kids there, many of them in gangs. They respected her because she had rules that she enforced always with love. Plus, she was a good head taller than any of them! Before that, she went to Biola when the "institute" was downtown and engaged in pranks like mine in college, but on a lighter scale. Glenda was raised on a family orange farm near Porterville where she was her father's right hand "boy" (that's what he used to call her). But Glenda was anything but boyish.

Tom grew up in San Pedro and sometimes went to sea on his father's tuna trawler. His dad had emigrated from Yugoslavia where fishing was the family business. Tom, who was tall and lanky, was a fine baseball pitcher, taking his high school team to the championship and also taking USC (University of Southern CA) to the national championship. He played pro ball for awhile with the Seattle Rainiers of the (now long-defunct) Pacific Coast League, then got an engineering master's degree and labored from then on in the aerospace industry. He helped design the booster rocket fuel tanks for the Saturn 5 Apollo Moon mission (he was a rocket scientist!) and was involved in the engineering related to many commercial and military aircraft, including one or two that I flew.

On most evenings, Glenda would have dinner available for us when I returned from Talbot after a day of classes. Most meals were not taken in their fancy dining room but at the cozy breakfast nook in the kitchen where we had a thousand sessions of fellowship as well as conversation about the church and political and aviation topics of the day. Around this table, Tom and Glenda infused me with much Christian wisdom and maturity that I was then lacking. At the church, they were my biggest supporters, and on any special occasion—birthday, graduation, etc.—they arranged festive parties at church or at their home.

I should also mention the many times that we went to their cabin at Hume Lake Christian Camp up in the Sierras not far away from Lemoore where I had served in the Navy. Glenda's dear mom and dad had previously owned the cabin. There, we'd usually attend to a small work project or two, take walks around the lake, enjoy Glenda's delightful mountain cuisine, and be illumined by the Christian theologians who would speak in the evenings. Once a trip, we'd usually descend via a winding road down to the bottom of Kings Canyon—a canyon I'd flown up and down a hundred times in the Navy (but not at low level)—and have a picnic lunch by the river. All very delightful and a blessing from God.

After I had been at Talbot for a couple-plus years and serving at Bethel Grace as the College-Career group director for about a year, American called me back to service. A part of me yearned to return to flying—even sidesaddle flying; another part of me felt that sacrificing the flying career for a pastor career would be the more spiritual thing to do. Compared to my adventurous life so far, I struggled sometimes to stay excited about the humdrum of everyday church life. Tom and Glenda advised me not to give up such a valuable thing for the time being: I could fly *and* do ministry, and I could switch to full-time ministry down the line if circumstances changed. So after much prayer and after acceding to some selfish desire to jazz up my life again, I returned to AA and, after training in Dallas to re-learn the flight engineer trade, went back to flying. But I continued my Talbot education, albeit at a reduced pace.

For the next two and a half years, my weekly schedule typically went like this: Talbot classes from Monday through Thursday; fly standby from LAX very early Friday morning to Dallas (usually I rode a first-dawn DC-10 flight that was always only half full); once in Dallas, commence a three-day work trip Friday, Saturday, and Sunday; after finishing the work trip on Sunday, return that evening standby to LAX; go to Talbot on Monday; rinse and repeat, etc. The Talbot homework was accomplished on the road at hotels in Atlanta, Chicago, Miami, Nashville, and New York. While the captain and crew were out having a good time on the town, I'd be back in my hotel room memorizing Greek and Hebrew words and grammatical concepts. That was difficult, but because I felt the Lord's call in it all, there was a certain satisfaction in it. The 727 FE job was good but far from perfect. I wasn't piloting, and American never used this jet type west of the Pecos, so all we ever saw was flat boring lands. All the while I yearned to fly over mountains again like I'd done in the Navy.

The chance for that came at last when I finished my MDiv, with decent grades, at Talbot in 1999. By then I was pretty much burned out on the flight engineer position, and I was now praying a lot concerning what I should do once I received my master's degree. *Should I keep flying? Should I quit and look for a full-time ministry position? Should I do something yet unthought of?* Then one night, in a powerful dream, the Lord, I believe, indicated a path that was unexpected and not entirely to my liking or ability. As I tell the dream, keep in mind how lousy a student I was growing up, that I was a slow learner, and although I'd done pretty well in seminary, I had to work at it probably harder than others.

In this dream I was trying with great difficulty to go up an awesome snow-covered mountain in my truck, Bob. I had the feeling that going up this dark and foreboding mountain had much to do with satisfying God's will for my life. Thinking I wouldn't have the traction to go up, I began to panic, but right then I saw a snow-free trail, got onto it, and was able to continue up. That trail where I got traction was "Harvard." Then I had the dream again, but this time when I first spotted the snow-free trail, I thought to myself, *Oh, there's Harvard University*, and was able again to get onto it and proceed up. Then I woke up, and even though it was still dark outside, it was time to get up for work.

Jimmer, my "bunkie mate," was still asleep in the upper bunk. As I took a shower, I thanked God for what I strongly felt to be a sign from Him but, at the same time, prayed half joking, half serious, that the Lord would miraculously provide me with clean underwear somehow—as confirmation. You see, when I'd gotten up and looked in my clothes drawer, no clean underwear was there. When done in the bathroom, I came out, started to go back into our room, and, to my surprise, there was Jimmer, up earlier than usual, standing there looking at me with a freshly-folded stack of piping-hot underwear in his hands—some were his, some were mine. Apparently Glenda had washed some the day before but not dried them. When I was taking the shower, Jimmer had gotten up and dried the underwear, folded them, and now presented mine to me. He had never done that before, and he never did it again. Just like the Lord had (maybe) caused that RIO to cackle long before, He had prompted Jimmer to dry and fold my underpants. All I could do was say "thank you" and praise the Lord! Jimmer had no idea of the significance of this.

Within a day or two, I related the dream to a more charismatic and older fellow student at Talbot. He reminded me of the couple of times in the Old Testament when men had double dreams that indicated that the symbolic meanings of the dreams would certainly come true. The lad Joseph, for example, had his double dreams that symbolized his family and others bowing down to him, and this sustained him during the next grueling twenty years after his brothers sold him into slavery. The dream eventually did come true but in a way that brought about the saving of his family and countless others. Maybe mine meant that I'd one day pass over Harvard in my old truck, Bob—"Harvard" probably at least figurative for higher learning, and "Bob" probably at least figurative of my normal mode of life—and some unforeseen good would come out of it.

I tell you these things now that I'm approaching the age when "the grasshopper drags himself along," but back then, I kept these signs that I took to be from God pretty close to my chest. Talbot was conservative and not charismatic (not "Pentecostal"). They generally taught that the "sign gifts" had melted away after the apostles of the Lord passed from the scene, and as a result, we now live purely by faith and not by direct interventions—through signs and miracles—of the Lord. As I learned more, I increasingly understood why mature Christians live by faith and not by signs, but I also could not find biblical justification for an absolute cessation of these gifts. While it may demonstrate the most excellent faith for Christians to make obedient and wise decisions based on God's Word (the Bible) and not crave signs that run the risk of testing God by demanding signs and by thinking poorly of God if He doesn't provide them, I don't think anything precludes God from using signs and miracles if need be. In any case, I had asked for a sign, and God (it strongly seemed to me) had answered His weak child's request. So, taking this as real and a signal to continue studying and maybe go for a doctoral degree, I explored the possibility of doing a second master's degree at Talbot, for it was generally understood then that one needed a master of theology if one were to pursue a doctor of theology.

The first order of business, however, was to transition from the flight engineer seat to the first officer seat (co-pilot) at American. So after graduating at Talbot with my MDiv and celebrating that at a poolside party at the Lovrich's, I took leave of the seminary for a semester and went back to Dallas to learn to fly the McDonald-Douglas MD-80. When I climbed into the FO seat for the first time and pulled the seat up, it was such a *good* feeling! The instrument panel layout was reminiscent of the Douglas A-4 Skyhawk, so I immediately felt right at home. The training went very well—I just reveled in the fact that I was flying again (admittedly then still in simulators), and my aviating skills, though five years stale, came right back. I asked to be assigned to the LAX base, and that's what I got.

My check ride in the real airplane went fine, although we hit a big goose just above the cockpit windshield going into Calgary late one night. It sounded like a shotgun going off in the cockpit. Fortunately, it didn't go into one of the engines. For the next three years, I flew out of LAX (no more commuting to Dallas!), went to class during the week, and in general loved life at that point because I was flying again, and I was beginning to pursue the very specific call of higher education. Plus, the flying was now around the rugged territory of the West Coast, which was wonderful. AA bought out Reno Air about that time, so we began flying all their old routes up and down the West Coast. I recall flying six legs a day on a few occasions and loved every minute of it!

As I was going through the ThM (master of theology) program, which was designed to precede doctoral degree studies, I had an eye on eventually doing a doctor of theology, but I had no idea where. Another consideration was the fact that many respectable schools required some knowledge of theological German. Because of the explosion of post-Reformation theological knowledge—both good and bad—that emitted from the German-speaking lands, schools around the world that offered doctoral degrees in theology or religion required some knowledge of that language.

Speaking of that, about this time I did a family history study that took me back east and revealed some amazing facts about my father's lineage on his father's side. I touched on that story at the beginning of this book. At the end of that study, I ended up flying over to London where I went to All Souls Church, thence to Munich on a British Airways flight on which I got the last standby seat. As I sat down, I noticed that the young lady sitting right next to me had a big Bible open in her lap. Her name was Irmgaard (Imri) and we had a lovely two hours together on the ride to Munich. Irmi would play a part in my initial German education not too long later.

As I continued to fly for American and do the challenging ThM, I wondered how I could continue to fly and do a doctoral degree, which all things combined, would surely be beyond my learning capability and industry level to do. I could go for a doctoral degree if I quit flying, but then how would I support myself? It was only as of late that I started making good money at American, so I didn't have much saved up.

The beginning of an answer came in the spring of 2002 when I was on a layover in Sacramento, CA. While out jogging near the layover motel, I saw a bird on a wire, then saw two birds, then one, then two. It quickly became apparent that I wasn't seeing two birds but seeing double. Not good. Over the following weeks, I noticed that sometimes my eyeballs wouldn't align, and I'd get double vision. Sometimes they were crossed and sometimes the opposite. Still I flew, but then on a one-day up and back to Reno and then San Francisco I realized that I was not fit for duty. LA to Reno during the day went OK. I flew the leg back with no problems, then the captain flew us up to San Francisco. But after dark when we took off over the black bay, with me at the controls with some turbulence, I got some vertigo and double vision. As we turned out over the even blacker ocean, I knew that if some malfunction added anything to the workload, I'd be hard-pressed to handle it. So once we got leveled off heading south, I told the captain my problem and gave control of the plane over to him. When we landed back at LAX and waited between the runways, he put his hand on my shoulder and prayed for me. That was the last time I flew for American Airlines.

I didn't know what was going on with my eyes and was quite worried about it, but not terribly so. Right away I sensed that God might be making a way for time to do my doctoral studies. For the time being, I had only called in sick but had not registered any official problems with AA. A little later, I called off the sick list and went to my yearly recurrent training in Dallas. When I was doing the same training the year before, jets of American and United hit the World Trade Center buildings, and I got stuck in Dallas. They put me over in the hotel where the flight attendants were stranded in order to provide pastoral counseling for the traumatized.

Now I was in Dallas again, trying to keep my cross-eyed act together in the simulators with all the usual bad weather and aircraft malfunctions. All went reasonably well, but when it came to the final simulator test—night landing at Reagan Washington National with an engine on fire and a short runway covered in ice—I slid off twice into the icy Potomac. The problem was that if there was one runway (like at DCA—Reagan), I'd see two. If there were two, I'd see four. If there were four (like at LAX), I'd see eight—which might have prompted me to ask the captain, "Which one do they want me to land on?" So to prevent this, I'd close one eye (I've worn an eye patch off and on ever since then), which meant that I'd see fewer runways, but I'd lose all depth perception at the same time and risk catastrophe upon landing where the margin of error is very slim.

In view of all this, I went back on the sick list right after I got back from Dallas and stayed there for several months until the doctors figured out that I had an immune system malfunction called myasthenia gravis (MG). This disease degrades the junctions between nerves and muscles and usually shows up first in the most precise muscles of the body: the eyeball muscles. MG typically generalizes into other muscle groups, but, thankfully, it hasn't done that so much with me. Unfortunately, the FAA considers the disease to be disqualifying, thus I was dead in the water. But I wasn't dead in God's sight! When I learned that I could fly no more, my first thought was, *Oh, so now the Lord has given me time to do my doctorate.* But on the heels of that thought came another: *How am I going to pay for that and support myself?*

Not long after, the AA flight operations office at LAX called me, and the secretary said in a chipper voice, "Where do you want us to send your money?" I replied, "What money?" She said, "Your disability money." Not realizing yet what was going on, I said, "You keep the money—I'll just go get another job." But she insisted, "No, Mr. Engleman, we contractually have to give you this money, so where should I send it?" In all that time with American I had no idea that the pilot union had negotiated, among other things, a provision that if a pilot became medically disqualified, he would receive an early pension till he came back or retired at normal retirement age. Suddenly the light came on, and it was as if the Lord hit me upside the head and said, *Hey, dummy, you wondered how I'll support you— this is how! Just take the loot!* So I gave the lady the info she requested and marveled at how God was paving the way for me.

Now that my wings were clipped for good, I was able to finish the ThM faster. By that time, the spring of 2003, I was getting a little bit embarrassed that I had been at Talbot for so long. For a man who never liked schooling, I sure spent a lot of time in school! Overall, my time at Talbot was excellent. The professors were all kind and super knowledgeable, and when I was the student body social chair for a year, they let me do just about every off-beat idea that came to mind.

The only mild discomfiture came with the quasi-psychology spiritual formation classes. Let me say a few words about this.

There seemed to be a tinge of Freudian perspective there as well as a slight frown on patriarchy. In one of the classes, the madam professor said that we would that day show humility and transparency by revealing some sin that had been encountered in the past. This would be most therapeutic. Most of the students in the class were relatively young Koreans, and one by one they confessed with trepidation, some with moist eyes, their sins that went something like this: "My father asked for a flat-head screwdriver, and I gave him a different one—oh shame." And another: "I went to a Christian retreat and had secret thoughts about one of the girls there—oh shame." And another: "I used my computer one night when my parents told me not to—oh shame." As I heard these and my turn came closer, I realized that I'd better come up with something relatively benign so as not to cause undue alarm. I don't remember now what I said, but whatever it was, the professor advised me soon thereafter to seek professional help.

During all that time at Talbot, nothing further occurred with Lilly, but I had a couple more dreams that I took as providential. In the first, I asked if we could talk; she said "no." Then I asked her out for coffee; she said "no." Then with less chance I asked her out to lunch; she said "no." Then with utterly no hope at all, I asked her out for a deluxe dinner. She said "yes." *Yes!?* I suppose one can be abruptly surprised with great ironies in dreams; on the other hand, they might be signs of outside influence.

In the second dream, I curled her little finger in mine in a gesture of profound love, and I said, "When I get back, we'll go on our first date." Then I woke up with a deep sense that it had been from the Lord. Was it? Or was it just me or maybe the proverbial pizza from the night before? So I continued to "wait upon the LORD" but also continued to ponder the possibility that He was using my flawed perception of all this to allow other ladies to pass by and thereby steer me toward what I then knew to be biblical—that is, toward perhaps becoming, as Jesus said, one of His "eunuchs for the sake of the kingdom" (Matthew 19:12). Plus, all my closer friends who knew about it believed that I was chasing the wind and advised me to get my head out of the clouds. Maybe I really did need help as the spiritual formation professor suggested.

From this point on in my education I was well outside the normal flow. Typically those who pursue doctoral degrees intend to teach, probably at the college level, as a profession and means of support. While working on their master's degrees, many students become teachers' assistants and through that gain introductions to schools and professors through which their doctoral degrees can be obtained. In the process some even produce books and journal articles. But by the time I thought about going for my ThD, I was already almost two decades into my aviation career and already past the age of forty. From the outset it seemed enough to learn some German and a little Latin if need be, participate some in pastoral functions at whatever church I might be at, and simply satisfy the minimum requirements for the doctoral degree. God would use it one way or another for His glory.

A year after I quit flying, I finally received my ThM. This was after a challenging oral test and thesis defense. Just before this, there had been a slightly embarrassing event. My thesis advisor, through formal invitation, invited me to have dinner with him and a top-flight Old Testament professor from another school. At the time I knew next to nothing about this OT professor, but I accepted. It was a nice time, but during the meal I knocked a glass of water into this professor's lap. Little did I know that several years later I would become familiar with his theological system and at a theological society meeting read a paper that strongly challenged this system (which caused feathers to ruffle amongst a few of his followers). The reason that I did this was because in Vienna I had tried to use his system myself and found it wanting. Seems the water in the lap had symbolic meaning that only in hindsight was discernable.

10

Climbing Mount "Harvard" in Austria

D one with Talbot, I set my sights on the doctor of theology. But where? In any case, as I understood, I needed to learn some theological German. I had been in contact with Irmi since meeting her on the Munich flight, and she suggested I come to her hometown near Augsburg. So that's what I did, but I first participated for two weeks at an archeological dig atop the giant Hazor Tel in northern Israel.

Things there got off to a bad start when one of my feet got tangled up with a big jellyfish while taking an evening swim at Tel Aviv. I got stung pretty bad, and my foot swelled up. Then, when the Hebrew-University-sponsored dig began, I realized that this dig was not about using dentist-type implements and brushes but pick-axes and shovels and buckets. To get down to the Middle Bronze Age of the Canaanites and Joshua's entry into the Promised Land, we first had to excavate down about seven feet in an area of some five hundred square feet. That's a lot of dirt! And it all had to come out by hand. But the two Jewish students from Hebrew University who led our group kept our extraction rate at very high efficiency. Mr.

Gordon Franz, who had been our lecturer on the first Talbot Israel trip, had invited me to this dig, and we roomed together while there. Every evening all would gather and "read" the pottery. One could get a PhD in that subject alone! Once the massive amount of dirt was removed, things did settle down to a slower digging rate. Lots of pottery was found, which is useful for dating layers, some jewelry, a few Egyptian scarabs (that showed that the Canaanites had relations with the Egyptians), and two Canaanite skeletons with short swords at their sides. When it was over, I was ten pounds lighter.

Leaving Hazor in a rented car, I went up to the Mt. Hermon ski lift (operating for tourists in the summer) and went to the top where a lady told us about the military outpost there. The view was fantastic—all the way from Damascus south to the Golan Heights—and the top of Mt. Hermon was only a few miles away on the Syrian side. Israeli soldiers could be seen guarding the border. There I met a young Jewish couple who invited me to picnic and swim with them later at the Jordan River. I accepted and had a delightful time. The next several nights were spent at an old YMCA hotel near Tiberias on the western shore of the Sea of Galilee. When the sun went down one evening, I bobbed in the perfectly flat Sea (with minnows nibbling on my toes) while a hazy moon rose in the East and prayed for all the brothers and sisters in my Sunday school class back at Bethel Grace.

My last stop in Israel was Jerusalem. There, one of my dig mates who had been an Israeli army tank commander made me dinner at his apartment. He was a good host, a good cook, and deadly serious when it came to issues of Israel's security. My last memory of Israel was sitting with another dig friend on the balcony of the Lutheran hospice at evening time, looking over the city and the Temple Mount while sipping on cool drinks and enjoying each other's company.

Once I got to *Deutschland*, Irmi was ready for me. She had me stay with the pastor of her house church and his wife, Udo and Maria, who turned out to be wonderful hosts. Days would be spent in Augsburg learning German and evenings with her at her beautiful rented house in Gablingin. This was my life for the next four months, and it was idyllic. Every morning the gracious Udo and Maria had some kind of breakfast for me, then I'd ride the train to Augsburg, participate in the very interactive class with students from all over the world, then ride the train back and hang out with Irmi and her Youth With A Mission (YWAM) friends during the evening. The German class was of the immersion type, and it was sink-or-swim, with hardly a word of English used. Once a week Irmi's friend Harry and I would meet at a small lake and slowly read through the German translation of the biblical book of 1 John.

In reality, all daily life then was *immersion*. To really learn another language, one has to be willing to be a fool and make lots of mistakes that the natives sometimes laugh at. For example, on one occasion with Irmi and her several girlfriends in a car, I spoke about how many Germans were going to mosques instead of churches. I thought I was using the right word for *mosque*, but it turned out I was ignorantly speaking a close-sounding word for a female reproductive organ. My worry about Germans going to mosques and doing such-and-such in mosques soon had the girls laughing uncontrollably. Later Albert, my landlord in Vienna, would berate me terribly for pronouncing "ö" like "o" (although he did save me from further great embarrassment after I'd been there for some time when he told me that the words I used for "Let's go for a walk" are only to be spoken to dogs!).

On the other hand, the only person who ever got really mad at me for one of my foolish language mistakes happened to be the conductor on the train back to Gablingin right after my first day of German class. He looked at my ticket, then looked at me and really chewed me out, then went off in a huff when I tried to respond in infantile German. I couldn't understand him at all. A little later I told Irmi about the incident. She looked at my ticket and laughed out loud. Turned out I had bought the less expensive *kinder* (children's) ticket.

It didn't take long for the primordial breezes of attraction to nudge Irmi and me into a warm friendship—something that I had resolved to avoid before I came. But the idyllic atmosphere and Irmi's qualities overcame my resolve for a brief time. Irmi's father and brothers lived nearby on the egg farm where Irmi grew up. She understood my love of chickens, and we were amply supplied by the farm for the many meals that she cooked as well as the several out-of-this-world apple strudels that she baked while I was there. The many evenings spent at her cottage by the gently-flowing *Schmutterbach* that spanned the warm late summer to the snowy chill of early winter were heavenly. But the mission, and all it entailed, were ever in the back of my mind. Because of that, I increasingly perceived as time went on that Irmi's intense dedication to YWAM—and encouragement for me to be involved in it—would not fit into my "Harvard" vision. Thus, just before Christmas I departed lovely Gablingin and returned to the States. Before I flew away, she cried bitterly. I really hurt her. I should not have let myself go, although the relationship was not immoral. In the twenty years since then, I have never again kissed a woman. I will forever be grateful for Irmi's wonderful hospitality.

Back then, I could still fly standby on American and associated airlines for very little money, so it wasn't that big a deal to go back and forth to Europe. My time in Germany showed me how little German I knew. The learning rate was so frustrating, unlike with younger minds. To learn a word, I'd have to use it again and again over many days, and then maybe it would stick. Thus I thought I needed another dose of German immersion training, but not in Augsburg. So where? After surfing around for some days on the internet, I found a school in *Wien* (aka Vienna) that was not too expensive and used the same curriculum that the Augsburg school had used. So I signed up for a class and also, through a Wien real estate website, arranged to meet a man who had a room to rent near the city center. As for details with all this, I knew next to nothing.

On a rainy and muggy spring afternoon, I entered Wien via train and *schleppte* my bags to the musty, old, and poorly lit coffee house where I was to meet the man with the room. I was jet-lagged, tired, and wet. The man, Herr Albert von Morawitz, showed up with his scroungy *Schäferhund* (German shepherd) a little later. After identifying one another (I was told he'd have a dog), the large man removed and shook off his trench coat, did the same with his Leninesque wool cap, ordered Zeppy to lie on the floor, and sat down. I didn't know it at the time, but he had somewhat of an unhappy socialist mindset and some traces of the classic *Wiener Schmäh* to boot.

Our first conversation was matter of fact. "*Also* [OK]," he said, without any pleasantries, "*sie brauchen ein Zimmer* [you need a room]?" "*Ja, ich brauche ein Zimmer*," I replied. But with that he could easily discern that my German was lacking, so, with some impatience, he switched to good English and clarified that he had an available room. It was very small but, being one building removed from the main street, was very quiet. The rent would be so much, and his only requirements would be that I pay and keep things "tidy." Having no other options, I agreed to take the room for at least the minimum time required.

We then finished our coffee, and he took me to his apartment that was on the top floor (seven or so floors) of an old building that his family had owned for several generations. The apartment had the look of being owned and maintained by a lifelong bachelor, and my room was indeed very small, but as it turned out, it was very quiet and perfect for what I was about to do. Albert had built a bed into the ceiling, so nocturnal sleep was reached by climbing a ladder and getting in position between ceiling and bed in such a way as to minimize claustrophobia.

Other than Albert watching TV in bed till late at night, all was quiet enough for ongoing studies. And even though Zeppy turned out to be as grumpy as his master, our regular times together as I jogged through Wien turned out to be enjoyable enough. After a few days, I agreed to stay there the three months of my German language course and Visa duration but at the time had no idea that I would be there again for a much longer length of time.

The language school was much like the other but with more students from the "eastern block" as well as Ukraine. My plan then was to complete the German course, then go to France for a little while to learn a few words of their language, and in the meantime figure out what schools I might apply to, domestic or foreign, for the doctor of theology. Wien had a rich history as a center of commerce and culture as well as military struggle between the Germanic west and the Ottoman east. The enormous Saint Stephen's *Dom* (cathedral) was at city center and always open to the public. I prayed there many times and once saw Handel's "Messiah" performed there by orchestra and choir.

About five blocks away from St. Stephen's was the much smaller and newer Protestant Vienna Community Church, which was English speaking. Although I knew this place would be somewhat more liberal than what I was used to, I decided to hang my hat there for awhile due to its nearness to Albert's and its location among all the shops and restaurants near city center. For those three months, it turned out to be a blessing, and several of the people there were very kind. One of these was Hilda Mwathi, originally from Kenya, who worked as the personal secretary of the head of the IAEA (Int'l Atomic Energy Agency) division of the UN. Another was Sita Weinrich who for decades had served in NGOs (non-governmental organizations) helping the women of Eritrea, a small nation next to Ethiopia. Both Hilda and Sita did much at church and offered wonderful hospitality while I was there.

One Sunday a guest preacher from the university filled the pulpit. When I heard that he was from South Africa and the dean of the school's Protestant Old Testament department, my providence-detecting antennae were tickled. I had already by coincidence strolled by the Protestant faculty on a walk with Zeppy (he led me there, as he was always out front on the leash), but the building that housed the faculty was old and run down. Dr. Alfred Loader seemed like a nice enough man, and his sermon was pleasant. Because of this encounter and my circumstances, and because I was already sensing in my sprit something special about Vienna, I decided to contact him a few days later. This being the grand old university that produced men like Christian Doppler, Alfred Edersheim, Sigmund Freud, Theodor Herzl, Ernst Mach (Mach 1.4 was my fastest!), and even the Reformation's Ulrich Zwingli, it was with fear and trembling that I made my enquiry. I assumed they would only scoff at a man like me.

After figuring out the right school email address, I sent Dr. Loader a message telling him a bit about myself, that I was looking for an OT doctoral program, and that I was wondering if studying there might be possible. A day or two later, to my amazement, he responded. Anxiously I opened the email and read his message, which went something like this:

Dear Mr. Engleman,

Of course you would be welcome here at the Protestant Faculty. . . . In fact, a countryman of yours has recently begun the same program, and you could join him.

As soon as I read that, I got down on my knees right there in the internet café and thanked God profusely. You see, I had assumed all along that it would take years to research and apply to doctoral programs and that the chances of admittance would be slim to none. So at this moment, I sensed that God had miraculously provided. Later events would show that He in fact did.

Soon after, I met with Dr. Loader at his office in the musty old Protestant faculty building. I specifically asked him if I could "be myself" and pursue the program as an evangelical Christian, and he said that would be fine. He also checked to see if Biola met their accreditation standards, and it did. Because I was soon going to complete the German immersion program, he suggested that upon return to the States I continue improving my German, take a couple of Latin courses, and make formal application to Universität Wien. If I were accepted, he would be my *Doktorvater.* I concurred with this course, said *auf Wiedersehen* ("till we meet again"), and not long after flew back to Los Angeles where I did all that he requested.

After taking German and Latin classes in the fall semester at UC Long Beach (and regular overnights and meals at nearby Tom and Glenda's), I got word that I had been accepted into the program at Universität Wien—but contingent upon my ability to pass a German fluency test once I got there. If I had been much younger the language would have come much quicker, but as it was, in my upper forties, learning that which comes miraculously for toddlers and children had for me been a giant mountain to climb. Thus I felt that I still did not have what it would take to pass the language test, and in any case, I would flounder in the many required classes all taught in German. I then told Dr. Loader that I still felt nervous about my German, but he replied with something similar to this: "Herr Engleman, come now rather than later. It is better to learn to swim at the deep end of *der Donau.*" So just after the new year of

2005, I flew to Vienna and, in some fear and trepidation, jumped into the deep and icy channel of the Danube!

Albert and Zeppy offered quarters again, and I accepted once back in Wien. Badly jetlagged and in great anxiety over the prospect of failing the German proficiency test, I trudged through the sloppy city snow to the university administration building and waited in line with many other bundled-up new students who smelled (as I did) like wet sheep. Once at the head of the line, I nervously presented myself to the matriculation lady and prayed silently that I would understand her. She asked various questions in German and requested certain documents. After about ten minutes of back and forth and checking computer files and such, she handed me an official-looking card. I asked (in German) "What is this?" She replied, "That is your student ID." Confused, I said, "But what about the German proficiency test?" She looked above her glasses and said with a slight smile, "The Protestant department told us not to worry about it. Welcome, Herr Engleman, to the University of Vienna!" My jaw hit the floor as she motioned for me to step aside and make room for the next customer. Then I went back outside into the snow and lifted my arms up to heaven in joy and praised God for this tremendous relief. I had worried about this proficiency test so much it almost made me sick. Then, poof! It was gone. My joy nearly instantly turned to mild panic, however, when I realized I would soon be in classes taught in German. Well, the Lord had provided all this way, and He would provide there too.

Before things got started, I had a cyst on my waist become inflamed. The same cyst had done the same thing almost two decades before in the Navy. Then, doctors on the ship simply lanced it, and man did that hurt. But this time it was about ready to explode. In the *Yellow Pages* I found a nearby clinic and trudged there through the snow on a gray day and got into a line that went out the entrance. Austria is a land of socialized medicine, so one must often wait for service. After a half hour or so, the line moved up and I came into the clinic. Once inside, I slowly noticed the strange paintings, or prints, hung on the walls that portrayed mostly nude bodies. Some twenty minutes after that, my position in line slowly moved past a medical brochure stand that was filled with literature about sexually transmitted diseases, and all the persons depicted on the literature were men. A depressing thought entered my head, so I looked up and down the line and realized that only men were there. The light would have come on sooner if I had not been in such inner focus on my pain. Right then a doctor came out of a room just behind the receptionist and, while walking to another room, recognized someone in line, smiled, waved, and said something in German with a completely international "flamer" style. Depression and revulsion came upon me at that point. I wasn't in the mood for this at all. But I was now, after nearly an hour, at the head of the line, and the receptionist said, "*Kann ich dir hilfen?*" I, in pain and despondency, said, "*Nein, danke,*" turned around, and exited the clinic back out into the gloomy gray and snow.

I endured the pain for several more days until the pastor of the Vienna Community Church recommended a nearby private clinic. Austria in general has universal healthcare. In addition, however, there are completely private clinics and hospitals here and there that can provide care quicker and with more personal attention, but you have to pay for it. Fortunately the insurance that AA still provided paid for the surgery to remove the cyst, and I finally had relief.

From time to time I would visit friends in the giant Wien AKH (*Allgemeines Krankenhaus*) socialized-care hospital and marvel how machine-like the facility looked, both inside and out—somewhat reminiscent of the Navy ships I had been on. It did, however, have many enormous murals on the walls of the endless passageways, but they were all unsettling depictions of nothing recognizable— modern art that gave no solace to the soul (a consequence of atheistic socialism). On the other hand, the private hospital that solved my cyst problem had soothing scenes of nature on the wood-paneled walls, and the chapel there was obviously built and furnished by people who love the Christian faith.

When my first classes came, I was pleased and greatly relieved to discover that I understood enough German sufficient to follow the general flow of thought. Another miracle! Sometimes I only recognized occasional words, but between that and my pre-class preparation, it was enough to get me by. During my five years there, Dr. Loader taught most of the classes, and, because he was a non-native speaker, he was easier to understand than the other professors. The classes consisted of some of the same subject matter that I'd covered in seminary, but now there were, in addition, smaller group seminars in which we presented and critiqued each other's ideas. These were especially hard to participate in, as my grasp of the topic under discussion at any given moment was fragmentary at best. This was because of the complexity of the subject matter as well as my limited knowledge of the language. In one seminar, I read a paper that I had prepared and, in the discussion afterward, heard several times the word *lächerlich*. I wasn't familiar with this but assumed that it was based on the similar sounding word *lecker*, meaning "delicious." They thought that my ideas were delicious, and this encouraged me greatly. But some time later I happened to stumble upon the word in a lexicon and was dismayed to read that it means "ridiculous" or "laughable."

As I somewhat knew beforehand, the worldview there at the Protestant department was based upon the assumption of naturalism and not supernaturalism. That is to say, the school, like many if not most western schools of all stripes, assumed that all phenomena, including religious phenomena, arose through naturalistic forces. Supernatural causation is not permitted. This is a pillar of modernity. There really was no God, for example, that spoke to Abraham, Isaac, and Jacob, who were the fathers of the subsequent nation of Israel; the proto-Israelites (whoever they were) *evolved* to the point at which they questioned their own existence and, as a result, felt like there must be a super-man ("God") out there somewhere who made them. Judaism and Christianity thus arose not out of God's creation of man but out of man's creation of God. Most if not all public colleges and universities in Europe and the US assume naturalism. Departments at these schools that prepare men and women for Christian ministry (departments of religion or divinity) have this perplexing disconnect that they send out graduates to lead the church yet do not really believe that the biblical foundation upon which the church is based is truly from God.

Nevertheless, because these schools today find themselves in the milieu of postmodernity, there is some allowance for expressions of supernatural truth to be had—and that's how a fundamentalist like me could be tolerated at a school like the University of Vienna. Let me explain this for a moment. The modernity that flowed from the seventeenth century scientific revolution (Francis Bacon, Isaac Newton) put the emphasis on what can be sensed through the senses (sight, hearing, feel, smell, etc.) using helpful devices like microscopes and telescopes. Amoebas and galaxies can be seen and studied and are thus real, but God can't be physically seen or heard, so He is put on the sidelines as far as *knowledge* is concerned. This modern thought was not atheistic but somewhat agnostic.

Then in the eighteenth century, prominent thinkers (like David Hume and Immanuel Kant) decided that even what we perceive through scientific observation cannot be trusted as the way things really are. Yes, God can't be observed, so He is correctly not eligible for *knowledge*. But because the scientific data that we do know comes through the unreliable and mediate human senses, then we must get used to the fact that we really don't know anything—well, except for the "I think, therefore I am" knowledge that is indubitable. But we should scowl even at that. So modernity that doubted God turned to postmodernity that doubts God and everything else, except for maybe the "me" that all of us are, respectively, immediately aware of. If there is any truth anywhere, it's got to be in li'l ol' "me." Postmodernity, therefore, is the worldview that understands that several billion "me"s have their truth *and* therefore have their proper say. If everyone knows nothing, but we decide to have schools that teach something, then each "me" must be given the opportunity to tell his own unique story. When the schools some decades before were more in the grip of modernity, I probably would not have been tolerated.

In truth, however, Dr. Loader didn't just tolerate me but actively sought the best for me. He understood that postmodernity gave me a voice, but he, more than others at the school, had a heart for Christ and the church that manifested itself in his desire for me to write in my dissertation what I understood to be supernatural truth—just to do it in a consistently well-reasoned way and in consultation with other scholars dealing with the same subject. Despite the original commitment I got from him to allow me to "be myself," it was I who wandered away from that commitment for a short while.

I began my dissertation employing a postmodern method, thinking I could satisfy both Athens and Jerusalem. Down in the musty basement library of the department, I came across a book that introduced the "canonical approach" to scholarly biblical studies and thought I'd give it a try. Not long into it, however, I realized that this method was based on postmodern thin air. (I also discovered that the scholar into whose lap I had knocked the water a couple years before was a leading exponent of it.) So, fortunately, I rejected it, in the process losing about a hundred pages of dissertation, and started over from scratch and from a Christian fundamentalist standpoint. Dr. Loader tore out some of his hair during this diversion but was patient and much happier with my work when I presented a conservative thesis regarding the "fear of God" biblical concept and argued well for it.

Nevertheless during my entire time at the school, I was constantly aware of the general skeptical and unbelieving spirit that hung over the place like the constant gray overcast of the Wiener winter. This, along with the dissertation production grind, as well as the constant language struggles, made it such that I needed refreshment on a regular basis.

I received this once or twice a week on my walks through the *Wienerwald* (Vienna forest) in the rolling hills just west of the city. After school, I might visit a *bon-bon* shop or a vegetable stand in order to buy a snack and practice my German, swing by my room, then take the *Strassenbahn* (streetcar) that stopped just outside the front door to the end of the line. From there one could walk through the forested hills for many miles and on into the Alps if one wanted to. At the bottom of one of those hills, I'd occasionally grab a part of a fallen tree and drag it up to the top, which would take about twenty minutes. All my life I have fought my weight, and this was just one method of doing that. Austrians would sometimes ask me what I was doing, then walk away shaking their heads. When I finally left Wien, there was quite a large stack of logs at the top. I sometimes wonder if it is still there.

I'd usually visit a hillside meadow overlooking Vienna where, warmed by the late-afternoon sun, I'd lie down and doze off. After the nap, I'd pray some—mostly for persistence and eventual success at the university—then explore the forest further while there was still light. As the sun set, the cuckoo birds would commence their lonesome calls (I initially thought these were clocks, but Albert corrected me), and as the lights of the city appeared, I'd wander by a local woodsy *Gasthaus* and have a bowl of lentil soup, then return home on the last streetcar.

From time to time I would meet interesting people in the Wienerwald. One Austrian young man whom I walked along with for a couple hours confessed that he believed all that I believed regarding God and Christ and Christian religion, but he just couldn't in good conscience bring himself to accept salvation because he saw himself as too much of a sinner. I tried my best to get him to see that Jesus came and died for people just like him—but he just wouldn't have it.

Then there was the gorgeous Russian woman. It was a very cold day with ground and tree branches covered with snow and silent ice fog in the air. After about ten minutes of prayer in a snow-encased brush jumble, I came out and continued down the trail. So far that day I'd been all alone. But as I walked on, I heard snow-crunching footsteps coming up behind me. When that person caught up and was about to pass, the fur-lined hood turned my way, revealing a beautiful face. The woman asked me in good German but with a thick Russian accent what I had been doing in the brush back up the trail. I told her that I had been praying. She looked perplexed and asked what *praying* was. Well, I was happy to answer that, so I invited her to walk on with me, and as we did I spoke about God and Christian prayer. All the while she listened intently. Coming to a fork in the trail, my message to her in my mind yet incomplete, I invited her to continue on with me to the forest Gasthaus that was my destination. She accepted the invitation and for the rest of the walk and a little later over our bowls of soup, I was able to present to her the gospel of Christ.

Then there was the time I lost my cell phone while walking the Wienerwald. By mild miracle, I got it back when I met a dapperly-dressed older gentleman at a coffee house who had found it. Well, it wasn't exactly him who found it. As he was walking the forest trail, his Schäferhund had gone off the trail and come back with my phone in his mouth. Fortunately I didn't have the screen locked, so he called a church friend in my contacts list, and that person was able to notify me. Sensing the providence in it, I was able to speak to him a little bit too about my Christian faith. One Schäferhund (Zeppy) had led me to the University of Vienna, and another Schäferhund had led me, so to speak, back to my hopelessly lost cell phone. Yes, God can even use German shepherds to help his hapless sheep!

On a few occasions Albert and I went on more adventurous excursions. On one of them we climbed *Schneeberg* (Snow Mountain) just southwest of Wien and, despite it being a foggy day, made it to the top. Driving back, he patted the dash of his new car and said proudly, "She runs great, doesn't she?" Not five seconds later, the car's radiator exploded in a burst of steam, and the engine immediately overheated. So we came to a stop on the *Autobahn* (freeway) sixty or so miles south of Wien. As we were pondering what to do next, a violent thunderstorm hit and filled the highway shoulder with gushing water. After waiting a few minutes for the engine to cool down, we scooped up some of the water and put it in the blown radiator and limped down the road for a few miles until the fresh water steamed off and the engine again overheated.

The storm remained over us, so again after cooling down we repeated the process and got down the road a little further. As long as the storm kept up, we were able to make slow progress until we came to the outskirts of Wien a couple hours later. At that point, the storm stopped, and we left the car at a repair joint that Albert knew about. Somehow we got home from there, and later Albert returned to get his repaired car. Ever since then, every time I slap the dash of my car and say something like, "She purrs like a kitten!" or "Most reliable car I've ever owned" or something similar, I always have that incident with Albert in the back of my mind and cringe waiting for the worst.

Social life at the school was overall quite pleasant. The students, who were mostly undergrads, were friendly and some of them true believers. Because Austrian universities are almost free (even for me, another miracle!), and because there are only a few conservative but unaccredited private Bible schools, many young people who want to enter into church work do their college education at one of the state universities. Again, the strange disconnect that I just mentioned was, at least for me, always the elephant in the room—that is, that we were training for service to God in a school that really didn't factor in God as described in the Bible as a causal agent.

One thing I didn't mention above in describing the worldview of the school is that they did have a vague notion of God and would not claim to be atheists, but "God" only as it is manifested in the consciousness of man. Liberal (naturalistic) Christianity believes that the God *out there* (i.e., the God as described in the Bible) cannot be known, but the God *in here* can, and that is the God with whom we have to do. Liberal Christianity thus has a somewhat pantheistic view of God because God is expressed in the consciousness of ourselves as well as our consciousness of everything we experience around us. In all this the subjective "God" is brought up, and the objective God of the Bible is brought down, and with Him, the overall authority of the Bible.

Dr. Loader in that first email mentioned a "fellow countryman" who had started the doctor of theology program just before me. We met off and on when he was in town for classes. Jordan Sheetz was an amazing fellow before whom I stood in a little bit of awe. It was enough for me to simply do the school program alone, and even with that I struggled. Meanwhile, Jordan proceeded through this doctoral program while, at first, pastoring a church in Portland, Oregon, and later, while laboring as a full-time missionary in Austria. All the while he also had the responsibilities of raising (along with his esteemed wife Rachel) five children (one of them a special needs child) and speaking and teaching at various venues. His knowledge of the Bible was extensive and his grasp of the Hebrew Old Testament a hundred times better than mine. If that weren't enough, he would now and again participate in Austrian black-belt karate tournaments! Wow! Finally, interestingly enough, he had been a student of the theologian into whose lap I had knocked the glass of water some years before. So we had a lot to talk about. Jordan went on to teach at an evangelical seminary in the Netherlands, thence to pastoral ministry and seminary teaching back in Portland.

A master's degree student at the university, Patrick Todjeras, took a friendly interest in me right away, and we became good friends. That was a great encouragement to me then. Over the next four years, he and his newlywed wife, Naemi, provided many instances of hospitality and Christian love. On several occasions, Patrick took me on holidays to his childhood home in Amstetten where his blessed mom, Christinela, and his two younger sisters, Emmanuela and Patricia, showed me all kinds of loving hospitality. Patrick's parents were originally from Romania. Sadly his father died when Patrick was only seventeen, so the young man from that point on had to help support the family. Naemi was from nearby Traun where her MD father, Manfred Türkis, had a home-based general practitioner practice. Naemi herself was going through medical school, planning to follow in her dad's footsteps. On several special occasions, Dr. Manfred and his gracious wife, Michaela, opened their home to me and made me a part of their family. I was even a patient in his practice one day and was well cared for.

On another occasion Manfred arranged for a bus to take the family and their church to Prague, and I was invited along. That was my first time there. I didn't realize that the history of that great city was as amazing as Vienna and that it had been the true cradle of the Reformation (John Huss). While there, I broke off from the group one morning and visited a Jawa motorcycle dealer (Jawa used to make the famous CZ motocross bikes in the sixties) and then walked through an old Jewish cemetery. I found it interesting that not a few tombstones had the name "Engelmann" inscribed on them, but probably no relation.

The patriarch of the family (at least the portion that I got to know) was Michaela's father, Fritz Börner. All were humble and believing Christians, but Fritz was especially earnest in his faith as well as in his belief in the supreme authority of Christ and His holy Word. He put this on display one day, along with a dose of brashness, when he spoke his mind at Patrick's graduation ceremony at the university. The importance of studying religion *scientifically* had been mentioned by one of the professors during the ceremony, and as the proceedings were closed, Fritz took the stage and microphone and forcefully declared something to the effect that the *wissenschaftliche* (scientific, i.e., naturalistic) religion taught at the school was doing more harm than good. It was an awkward moment, and a brief debate ensued between the professors and Fritz. But what he said was true, and his willingness to mar protocol in order to make a memorable stand for truth was an inspiration to me.

In any case, Patrick and Naemi and their families went out of their way to add blessings to my several years in Austria, and for that I will always be thankful. Patrick would go on to be an Austrian Lutheran pastor and head an organization that helps churches present the gospel in culturally relevant ways. He also now leads a research center for missions and church in the German-speaking countries and teaches at the University of Zurich.

Back in Wien, things went pretty well overall for me at the Vienna Community Church (VCC). I preached on occasion and taught a Sunday morning Bible study at a nearby restaurant before church started. From time to time I was also invited to teach an ongoing Bible study at the nearby United Nations complex. When there, I'd sometimes rent a rowboat on the adjacent *Alte Donau* and get an upper body workout rowing up and down that waterway. Toward the end of my time at the VCC, I led a new midweek Bible study that was at first well attended. But when the subject of sexuality came up, and I showed what the Bible says about homosexuality, everyone drifted away. Right about then, the church finally got a new pastor, and he was all for homosexuality and homosexuals serving in the church. I was not willing to serve under a man who believed that. So I said farewell to everyone and thanked them for being so gracious to me the last few years, and I looked to hang my hat elsewhere.

There was another international church on the south side of town—the International Baptist Church of Vienna (IBCV). So I went there and immediately recognized it as being much more like the "old time religion" that I was used to. I stayed there until the program at the university was complete. Everyone there was very good to me, especially a devoted Christian couple, Mark and Irina Werth, who regularly showed me hospitality at their home. Mark was American but as an Army officer had met Irina, a German *Fräulein*, while on duty in Deutschland. They eventually settled in Bavaria but came for several years to Wien when Mark got a UN-related job that had to do with tracking military armaments in the various eastern-block and Slavic-speaking nations.

A family originally from Indonesia, the Racas, were also especially kind. The dad, August, was a professional cook at one of the high-end hotels, so when they had me over, man, the meals were out of this world. His son, Erwin, and his girlfriend, Nicolle (now married), and I sometimes led worship in the church and also played special numbers from time to time. Then, I played a twelve-string guitar that I had bought just after arrival in Wien (that same guitar often gets played in my California church today). There were others at the church—the Mangens, Fawunmis, Lojeks, etc.—who were very good to me.

During the doctoral program, I returned to the States several times in order to reorder my domestic affairs, see friends and Mom, and hit the Mojave Desert with my good friend Bob Miller. Bob, called by most "friendly Bob," first came into my life when he was hired by Tom and Glenda to do a paint job at their house. They invited him to Bethel Grace, and he and his wife, Teri, came and decided to stay a while. Bob had been a quasi-outlaw biker long before, then got saved and became an evangelist to fellow riders. No one was as good as he on a big old Harley, no one was as strong, and no one could soften the hearts of outlaws like he could and win them to Christ. About the time I went cross-eyed, I talked him into getting a used dirt bike. So he found a well-worn Honda XR 600, inscribed Colossians 3:12-13 on the gas tank with a heat gun, put a saddle bag on it, and made himself available. He named his bike "Meekness," and I named mine "Kindness" (my KTM 500 that I had since Navy days). About that time, someone gave him an derelict circa-1967 Dodge motorhome in exchange for a paint job. Bob, with much ingenuity and only a little money, got it going, and this proved to be our transport and camp headquarters on many excellent adventures over the next decade.

Several times before I went to Wien and several times on my trips back from there, Bob and I blasted off in "the Coach," with bikes and fuel and firewood in tow, and headed for the Mojave with Ginger the dog. On the first couple trips, his wife, Teri, rode along and did all the cooking, which was great as she was a super cook. Later when it was just Bob and me, I was pre-trip planner, coach co-pilot, off-road navigator, and camp cook. So I had to plan the menu, get the grub, and have everything staged when Bob got off work so we could split right away. Typically, though, I didn't have a particular destination in mind, but I let the Spirit move me as we headed up into the desert. Once we found someplace suitable—usually remote and well after dark—Bob would hoist the Christian flag and unload the bikes while I made dinner. Initially the plan was for me to cook and for Bob to do the dishes. But after the first trip or two, I took his job too—reason being that he then delegated the task to Ginger, who, admittedly, did clean things up quite nicely. Nevertheless, I told him (and Ginger) to relax by the fire and I would take care of everything.

Our daily routine was usually the same: get up at sunup, make and eat breakfast, do a Bible study and prayer, ride and explore the desert till near sundown, cook and eat dinner, go to bed, and repeat for the next two or three days out. The riding consisted of simply exploring the valleys and mountains of the Mojave while stopping regularly to sip on hot coffee or have a snack or take a photo or two of the magnificent vistas. Between getting there in the dilapidated Coach and exploring the remote desert on old dirt bikes, we were typically flying on a wing and a prayer.

On one of these trips back home (December 2007), I rendezvoused with a friend who knew Lilly and who said that she'd been asking about me. Needless to say I was surprised and sought further information. Well, one thing led to another, and Lilly and I had a brief email exchange (which, after fourteen years of waiting, amazed me), and then we went for a walk up the creek that flows through Biola. She was as nervous as I was. I couldn't help but think in terms of the possibility that God was finally fulfilling what I took Him to indicate long before.

Over the next few weeks we got together several times. We hiked to the top of San Gabriel Peak where I had begun my Biola experience; we spent a day in "Bob" exploring the San Gabriel Range in the snow; she helped me prepare a dinner for several of us, including a German exchange student going to Biola; and we hiked the hills above Biola where I had hiked numerous times before and prayed about her, and I told her about some of the ways that I believed God had spoken to me about her. One of the most pleasant memories was of several occasions driving down the road in Bob singing hymns. In her lap was a large hymnal that contained not only the lyrics but a short biography of each hymn writer as well. But after all that, she said to me one night, to my surprise and some disappointment, that she did not have romantic feelings for me. Finally, she took me to the airport to return to Wien, and just as we said goodbye, she gave me a gardener's kneeling pad to take along. I had been complaining how my knees got sore when I prayed. I still have that pad and still use it as she intended.

Once I was back in Wien, however, she, via email, began expressing a growing tender love for me. We planned that in the summer she would fly over, and I'd show her around the grand city. Unfortunately not long before she came, she was told by a trusted common friend that our relationship was unrealistic. This hurt Lilly, and she wanted to cancel the trip, but I talked her into coming. When she arrived, I sensed that she was somewhat distant, but I had a pretty good time showing her the city nonetheless. On the third day of her week-long planned visit, we sat by the ornate *Gloriette* overlooking the royal flower gardens and *Palais Schönbrunn* of the Austrian emperors. Here she chose arguably the most romantic place in the world to tell me that she didn't love me. She flew back to LA a couple days later, earlier than planned. But in that short time, I did learn more about her. Between what seemed to be a so-so interest in me, as well as our soul issues that weighted us both, the possibility of long-term attachment was remote.

A year or so later, I did see Lilly briefly again in LA, but she was clearly not interested. Her last words to me as we parted were, "I'll see you in heaven." Right after that meeting I grumbled harshly before the Lord but soon repented. There's been no communication with her since then. So I've learned my lesson: putting too much emphasis on a heavenly sign can slip into doubting God's goodness (and thereby testing Him) if I don't get the sign I want or, if I do get the sign, doubting God's goodness if the fulfillment of that sign is not what I expect. Having said all that, let me say this: I still believe that God was in it somehow. He loves us, knows our situations intimately, and meets us where we are at in our journey with Him. In my (albeit immature and somewhat impure) good-faith effort to follow Him, I don't believe that He would have allowed me to walk these long paths (Biola, Lilly, "Harvard") unless His hand—however mysteriously and inscrutably—were somehow in it. And doesn't the Holy Bible tell us (1 Thessalonians 5:20; 1 Corinthians 13:7) that love "believes all things," and that while prophecies are inferior to love, still, we should not "despise" them?

Over one of the summers in Austria, I took a break from Albert and spent a couple months at an old hotel at the ski resort of Semmering. Getting there involved a scenic train ride through the medium-sized mountains of the eastern Alps. Overall, it was quite a nice time. After visiting a bakery in the morning, I'd usually study most of the day and then take a long walk on the ski hill in the evening. The hotel restaurant had a big fish tank in which swam big fat rainbow trout. Yes, indeed, all-American rainbow trout! Rainbows are not native to Europe, but the last kaiser of Austria imported some from California when he learned that they are more robust—and therefore more commercially productive—than the native *Bachforellen* (creek trout, aka, German brown trout). I'd point to one of the trout in the tank, and the waitress would fish it out and pass it to the chef. Then it would show up on my table twenty minutes later. On one of my walks, I happened upon the primitive fish hatchery whence these trout came. At that time there was actually a growing "green" movement to reestablish the native browns in the creeks and rivers and get rid of those *Auslander* (foreign) rainbow trout. They still tolerated me, however. (I never told them I was more of a *cutthroat!*)

Just before coming to Semmering, I woke up one morning with the sixties war film *In Harm's Way* powerfully on my mind. This came out of nowhere since I had not seen the movie nor thought about it since about 1968 when it was shown on TV, and it then made quite an impression on me. Sensing something providential in it, I looked up info about the movie and found that the director, Otto Preminger, was Jewish, now deceased, and had grown up in Vienna and narrowly escaped the Nazis when they came to Vienna just before the war. *Isn't that interesting,* I thought.

About a week later in Semmering, while taking an evening walk, I met a friendly elderly couple who invited me to have dinner with them at the nearby mountain *Hütte* (class of primitive restaurants scattered about the Alps). They were both Jews. Over the nice meal, Bernard told me how he had escaped Vienna just as the Nazis came in, and he by various desperate means had finally made it to Israel where he served in the British Navy till the end of the war, at which point he returned. He had only harsh words for the Austrians who by and large collaborated with the Nazis. Few of his relatives survived that Holocaust. I then mentioned that I had just read about the film director Otto Preminger and that he had also barely escaped. Bernard, surprised, exclaimed, "Oh, he was my cousin!" With this, I felt like the Lord was saying something, perhaps as He had done before, about the Jewish people. So I told them a little about my faith in Christ and later prayed for them several times. But I never saw them again.

At the third year point in Wien, I decided to move. Albert and I got along pretty good, but he was an atheist and thus I endured an ongoing atmosphere of mild mockery regarding my faith, which I figured was the cost of doing business. A day came, however, when he said something terrible about the virgin Mary, and that pushed me out the door. For the next few months I lived in a campus dorm, then moved about thirty miles from town to an idyllic Wienerwald village called *Weissenbach*, and there rented a small room at a working farm (*Pension Edlahof*). Through the autumn and snowy winter I holed up there in that cozy nook and wrote the rest of my dissertation. Every morning Frau Reischer would make me breakfast, usually for me alone, but sometimes for another guest or two, and after that I'd spend the day reading and writing. Before sundown I'd take a walk through the forest and pray at some suitable spot.

While going cross-country on one occasion through deep woods, I came to the edge of a small clearing and suddenly heard a man yelling something from the other side. Turned out he was in a hunting blind up in a tree, and unbeknownst to me, the hunting season had just begun, and I had almost become his first "buck!" When I got to the blind, the fellow really chewed me out, and I promised to be more careful. Hunting there is a quasi-religious activity where the hunt is initially blessed by the local Catholic priest, and the cross between the antlers is the symbol of the season. Weissenbach was at the end of a spur train line, so when Sundays or class days came, I could easily ride the train (with a connection or two) to Wien. It was a challenging yet magical time. A part of my heart was left in that charming place—if just for the reason that big fat German browns filled the creek that flowed through town. (I never caught one; to get a fishing license there takes an act of the Austrian parliament!)

Toward the end of that winter, I apartment sat in *Mödling* for a sweet missionary couple, Jeremy and Heidi Mullin, who took leave in the States for three months. And then for a similar period, I did the same in *Baden* for a couple, Carl and JoLynn Krause, who had an effective marital counselling mission in Austria and Ukraine but based in the US. While in Baden, my dear California church friend Lance Saltzmann visited for a couple weeks. We rented an Audi A4 and toured all over Austria and southern Germany. Lance knew some German, so I tried to get him into as many conversing opportunities as possible. We had a good time together, but the day I turned the Audi in, I happened to look closer at the gear shift knob and realized that there was a sixth gear that I had never used. All along I thought it was a five speed. I just had to shake my head. Even still, the gas mileage of that car was outstanding.

My last formal place of lodging during my "European vacation" was again in downtown Wien with a man from our church, Mr. John Janett, who was somewhat older than me and who worked by day as a principal at an international Christian school located near the UN complex. My dissertation by this time had been submitted (after much back and forth with Dr. Loader), and all I had to do was get ready for the dreaded *Rigorosum* where Dr. Loader and other profs would grill me on my dissertation and other pre-arranged subjects.

Living with John in his apartment was fine, although cramped. John was likable and hospitable, and he did a world of good for the children at the school by teaching them both earthly and heavenly wisdom. He did have a few quirks, though. For example, he would set his CD player alarm clock to blast out Elvis's "Ain't Nothin' but a Hound Dog" at 4 a.m., and then he'd take five minutes to pour a bowl of cereal while I was still in bed on the kitchen couch. I'm just poking fun now. Truth is we had a good time together, and I thank John for being so kind. One fine thing we did for that couple months was go over to the Raca's once a week and teach a Bible study after dinner. All the family was there every time, and it was such a blessing for all.

When it came to the last month's cramming preparation for the Rigorosum, I flew the coop again and went to a rustic hotel at the base of Schneeberg (that Albert and I climbed a few years before). It was now winter again, and the hotel and surrounding forests and mountains were covered with snow. What I knew about the hotel was only what I'd seen, in German, on the internet: it was in the mountains near a train line to Wien, and they had their own restaurant where meals could be taken. Sounded good to me. It turned out to be the perfect place for the intense preparation for the showdown to come. Not only would I be interrogated about my dissertation thesis (that the emotion of fear is contained within the OT concept of the "fear of the Lord"), but also the lady psychology professor would be there to test me on Viktor Frankl's theories of meaning (he was a Holocaust survivor), and, lastly, the NT professor would probe the depths of my understanding of Romans chapters 9–11 where Paul explains how God's OT promises can be fulfilled by the Jews *and* the church.

The hotel turned out to be a lovely place, although the other guests—numbering about fifty—were not so sociable. I also thought it unusual that the staff sat me at meals a few tables away from the other guests. At first it crossed my mind that, being American, they believed I needed more space. On several occasions I tried to engage a few of the other guests in pleasantries, but they would look at me, then walk away without saying a word. After about a week, I told the owner of the hotel that I was having a delightful time but that I'd wondered why the other guests seemed a little bit hard to relate to. She looked at me curiously and said, "Herr Engleman, you don't know what kind of hotel this is?" I said, "It's just a *hotel*, isn't it?" Then she smiled and laughed and said, "No, Herr Engleman, this is a 'Kur' hotel for people with psychological problems. We believe in and carefully practice proper sedation." With that, the light came on. *Ahh, so that's it,* I thought to myself, then said to the manager, "But how did I get in here?" She replied that if they had extra rooms they would occasionally take in extra guests, assuming that they understood that it was a *psychologisches Kurhotel.* Apparently on the website I had missed this fact. All was good after that, and I had no problem communicating with them once I knew the situation.

Toward the end of my stay, the hotel took the Kur patients up to a nearby ski area to do some sledding, and they invited me along too. I got to know some of them better on the bus, and once on the slope, I encouraged them to loosen up and have a blast on the hill. They were hesitant and fearful at first, but once I demonstrated how it was done, they all eventually took to the sleds and sped down the hill with many whoops of joy. Sleds and snow are much better therapy than sedation.

After my pleasant winter Kur, I felt prepared enough for the Rigorosum. I'd heard rumors about it being truly rigorous and other rumors about it being more of a formality. I felt good now, but not long after moving in with John a couple months before, I suddenly felt terrible about my prospects of overall success. The reason why was this: Once the dissertation had been given a thumbs-up by Dr. Loader, it had to go to a second judge for approval. To my amazement and satisfaction, he let me pick the second judge, so I chose an evangelical scholar who I was sure would be sympathetic to my ideas. I didn't doubt for a second that he would give my work anything other than his heartiest commendation and that he wouldn't take long to give it.

After about two months still not hearing anything, I went to a Wiener internet café and checked my email for the umpteenth time, and there I found a message from Dr. Loader. Eagerly I opened it, but to my horror he told me that the other professor had flunked me. I couldn't believe it—my own flesh and blood shooting me down in flames! At that moment, I assumed that this was the end of the road; all the leading of the Lord and years of constant toil and hardship in a moment gone up in a puff of smoke.

Coming out of the café, I was so distraught that I desperately needed to find something, anything, to divert my shock. Across and just down the busy street was a multi-story city mall, so I dodged cars and streetcars and went there and anxiously looked around. Immediately I spotted a multi-screen movie theatre and went up to the ticket counter and asked what movie might soon be starting. She sold me a ticket for the next one up, and I went in and found a seat and was "sedated" as I watched, for the next couple hours, *Ice Age II*. Worrying about what that frantic squirrel would do with his ever-problematic nut actually caused me to forget my own problems for a little while.

Soon thereafter Dr. Loader told me, to my great relief, that this was *not* the end of the line—at least not yet. In this case, the dissertation would go to a third judge but of his choosing, and that judge would break the tie, either yea or nay. So again I waited. Meantime, I read the critique of the second judge and came to perceive a couple of things. First, he had not read all of it nor understood its logic flow. This appeared to be partly because the German involved was indeed quite difficult. Second, not fully understanding my argumentation, he gave the benefit of the doubt to the German theologian whose standard work (about the "fear of God") I labored to refute. There is a tendency among some conservative scholars to over-admire the glorified scholars of the secular academy. I can't say if that was the case here, but I have been guilty of some of that myself. (The growing discernment of this eventually prompted me to write *The Slaves of Immanuel Kant*.) My dissertation did not really reveal anything new and was limited in its interaction with the scholarly literature—that is, it wasn't a great dissertation. On the other hand, the core argumentation was painstakingly well thought out and true and gave the public a long-overdue scholarly correction to a German work that many assumed was the gold standard.

The third judge, chosen by Dr. Loader, was a professor at the University of Budapest—a school much like Universität Wien. So I waited on pins and needles till I finally got word about a month later that she passed me—barely. But I was elated! I suspect that Dr. Loader might have oiled the gears a little bit behind the scenes, caring very much that, after all we'd been through, I would not return home despondent. So with this, I was cleared to proceed with the Rigorosum.

That day came right after I returned from the mountainside Kurhotel. After final preparation and prayer, I showed up at the department's new administrative office in the magnificent main university building and reported for the ordeal. Dr. Loader, Dr. Heine, and Dr. Pratcher were there. After offering me a *Tasse Koffee* (which I could hardly hold for shakiness of hand), they asked if I wanted to proceed in German or English. A part of me really wanted to do it in German, but I didn't want to put the whole enterprise at any undue risk, so I chose English. Dr. Loader began the questioning about points in my dissertation and after an hour or two was satisfied. Because the dissertation was about acquiring a true concept of the fear of God only by assuming the existence of God, this gave me opportunity to weave into the discussion the topic that I would next discuss with madam Dr. Heine—that is, that Victor Frankl's "psychology of meaning" could only have *real* meaning if God were there to give it meaning. Thus, when it came Dr. Heine's turn to question me, she was already satisfied by my knowledge of the subject already demonstrated in my answers to Dr. Loader.

Relieved by that, I next braced for a barrage of difficult questions about Romans 9–11 from Dr. Pratscher. But he only asked me one, and one that was completely unrelated to the assigned text but did remotely relate to the dissertation topic. He said, "Herr Engleman, Paul, in Ephesians, says that a wife should fear her husband. Do you agree?" I wasn't sure if this was entirely friendly. But the Lord, I believe, put a retort in my mind that helped neutralize the situation: "Ja, Herr Doktor, that is what Paul says. But if a husband cheats on his wife, shouldn't he fear her?" Dr. Pratscher seemed to ponder the reply, but Dr. Heine smiled and even chuckled a bit. He then said (to my amazement), "I have no further questions," and that was that. They then had me step out to the balcony while they conferred.

After a long ten minutes, they called me back in and congratulated me for passing the test and, as a result, for obtaining my "*Doktor der Theologie*" title. As was the custom, I had brought a bottle of not-so-cheap champaign, so we poured that into glasses and toasted, and I thanked them all and they wished me well. When I walked out of the building, it had been five years since I had first entered that building worried sick about the German exam. I couldn't believe that I was really done—and successful. God was very good to me, and I'm glad that I had a man like Dr. Loader to care for me the whole way.

The graduation ceremony wasn't till summer, so I took my leave and flew back to the good ol' U.S. of A. I escorted Mom and Jack

(Mom remarried a distinguished British gentleman about six years after Dad died) to Arizona for a little vacation and later to Scotland to visit some of Jack's family. This was all a lot of fun, and on top of all that, Mom bought me a new car as a graduation present! Meanwhile, I wasn't sure what the next vocational steps should be—I was already past fifty and doubted because of that if I was even hirable. Even if I was, would I have the energy for a full-time teaching job?

Another dose of reality was looking over the credentials of fresh young PhDs and ThDs being hired at colleges and universities and seminaries. They already had lengthy "curricula vitae" describing their many journal articles, books written, papers read, scholarly society memberships, and their "Phi Beta Kappa" and "Who's Who" identifications. Other than my master's thesis and my dissertation, I had none of that—except that single paper read at a theological society meeting a couple years before. Lastly I imagined myself in a school somewhere teaching basic classes that many others could just as easily teach, and then I pondered the possibility that God might want me to use my unique gifts in order to do some things that others could not do. But it wasn't long till I had to put all this on hold and return to Wien to graduate.

In July of 2010 I received my diploma—all written in Latin. Dr. Loader presented me the document, and I promised, like all others who graduate there, to support the school in the future. I still intend to do that when I go there some day to speak about the eternal price we are likely to pay when we exclude God *a priori* from our study of religion. Then I spent a few days tying up loose ends around Vienna and made preparations for a party for my friends. Up in the hills southwest of the city, I reserved an old hilltop restaurant with picnic tables outside looking over the forested countryside, and I invited everyone from the church, as well as Patrick and Naemi and their families, to come and have a good time a few days later.

Overall, my expectations were met or exceeded. The day was perfect, the dinner delicious, and the atmosphere as we watched the sunset delightful. The next morning, I met Patrick's and Naemi's families for breakfast, then a little later met Mark and Irina and a young German woman who came to our church, Franci, for a leisurely time together at the restaurant from the night before, sipping cool drinks and enjoying the view. But it was all over too soon.

A few days later, Erwin, Nicolle, Maureen, and I rode the train to Semmering, and we climbed the same ski mountain where I had met Bernard, the elderly Jewish man, and his wife a couple years before. We all made it to the top, huffing and puffing, and had lunch under the cross there, then returned to Wien quite exhausted. Maureen was a young girl in the Philippines when I had been there off and on in the Navy. I didn't know her then, but our time of serving the church together in Wein was indeed a blessing.

My last hurrah in Austria was with the aforementioned Franci. She invited me to visit her at *Neusiedler See* (lake) and do some biking and swimming. Franci had been working as a nanny for a family in a nearby town and wanted to do something nice for me before I left for good. We had worked together on various group projects at church, and I appreciated her as an honest and friendly Christian woman. So I rode the train down to this large shallow lake on the Hungarian border, and there we leisurely bicycled along the endless shore, then later went for a relaxing swim in the placid waters. It was all very pleasant.

In the evening we had a nice dinner on a restaurant balcony overlooking the water and the setting sun. As the sun declined closer to the horizon, and as some wine inclined our souls toward sweeter fellowship, my heart was warmed as we conversed about all the good times of the last couple years, and the feeling increased as the sun in all its glory touched the surface of the *See* and began to hide itself behind the earth. Just as the last bit of the sun disk disappeared amidst the romantic orange glow spanning the western sky, I felt my hand move involuntarily towards hers. But just before it got there, it seems the God of all nature commanded, *That close and no further!* by instantly unleashing a massive swarm of bloodthirsty mosquitos. It was so bad, all we could do was grab our stuff and run for cover! We made it back to her car with bites all over us. But then I looked at my watch, and to my amazement, the time had gone by so fast that I was about to miss the return train. So we sped to the station and said a hasty goodbye, and I ran to the platform just in time to catch the last train to Vienna. *A pitiful case, am I not?* At all events it was really sweet of her to send me off with such a lovely time.

The entire time in Wien, with the pressure of the school program always upon me, I had now and again daydreamed about the day when I would look out of the rear window of the last car of the train and watch Vienna recede into the distance. That day finally came, and I, almost in a surrealistic frame of mind, took that train and in the rearmost car watched the city fade away. Right then Maureen called me on my "handy" to tell me goodbye, but as we talked a little more, the cell signal was lost as the train entered the hills west of the city.

After several train connections I ended up at Grindelwald in Switzerland at the base of the towering *Eiger* (Ogre) mountain that many climbers had tried to climb, and not a few had died. On the second day there I hiked a narrow trail along the bottom of the Eiger's gigantic northwestern wall and there found a carabiner, ironically made in America, that some climber high above had accidently dropped. Ever since then, I've used it as an anchor to secure a saddle bag to the front fender of "Kindness." The trail ended at the hotel/restaurant where people watch the climbers with telescopes and where several scenes of Clint Eastwood's *The Eiger Sanction* (that I saw at Clark College many years before) were filmed.

My plan upon leaving Grindelwald was to go to France and visit the city of Nancy just so I could tell Mom that I'd been there. But I just missed the last train there when I got to a station near Strasbourg, so, not knowing what else to do at midnight, I slept on the train platform. The next morning as the sun came up, somewhat chilled and tired, I changed my mind about France and instead headed to Stuttgart and the international church that Mark and Irina Werth now attended (they'd left Wien about a year before when Mark's UN-related work ended). It was Sunday, and I arrived in time for the service, looking and feeling somewhat like a homeless person.

It was wonderful to see the Werths again. In addition to them, Darryl Bock, a well-known evangelical scholar, was there (he would do research during his sabbaticals at Tübingin University and lodge with Mark and Irina while there). Patrick and I a couple years before had taken Darryl to dinner in Wien while he was there for the international meeting of the Society of Biblical Literature, and just before that I had first met him when he visited the Werths at their house in Wien.

At the end of the service, I mentioned to Dr. Bock that I had it on my heart to take a whack at that horrible wall that keeps God out of public life by writing a critique of Immanuel Kant's monumental "critical" philosophy. In response, all he said was, "We're not going back." By this I think he meant that the "signs of the times" indicate that Christ will return before there is a return to anything remotely resembling Christendom. He would know better than I, and I tend to agree. Yet in the following years that heart burden would continue to nudge me on such that I eventually would write that critique (*The Slaves of Immanuel Kant*) and publish it (in 2023). If we are indeed "not going back," I hope at least that the Lord in that day will give me an *attaboy* for doing my best to show that the emperor of modernity and postmodernity (i.e., Kant) never in fact had any clothes.

After a day or two at Mark and Irina's, I had a couple days to go till my flight home, so I looked at a map and randomly picked a destination between Stuttgart and Munich on a spur train line called *Schelklingen*. Once there I found a small Gasthaus and settled in. Between the long walks and hospitable people, it was a very nice time. The best thing there, other than the people I met, was a beautiful spring near a protestant private school. Perfectly clear blue water came up silently out of the deep bottom of a pool that was about a hundred feet across and more or less round. One evening while there was still a bit of light, I laid down with my eyes next to the water, looking across the pool. The surface was perfectly still and flat, there being no breeze at all. Then I took my finger and very gently touched the water surface with the tip and pulled back and watched what would happen. The light and reflection off the water was such that I could see everything that then occurred. From that point of the slight dip, little waves went out in all directions, including toward the other side. The very first ripple hit the far shore at about the thirty second mark and bounced back, heading toward me while pushing through the many tiny waves that were still heading out. That first wave after about another thirty seconds arrived back at my shore, then bounced again toward the far shore. Within one minute there were thousands of ripples going all which ways all over the pool, and this kept up for a long time.

I've told that story many times over the years as a metaphor of how God can take our little efforts on Christ's behalf and multiply them "far more abundantly beyond all that we ask or think, according to the power that works within us" (Ephesians 3:20). We only see the first ripple or two, and maybe not even that. But God sees the ripples far down the line and can supernaturally magnify them—all to His glory. If we serve Him in honest faith, He will do this because He promised that He would. "For the eyes of the LORD move to and fro throughout the earth that He may strongly support those whose heart is completely His" (2 Chronicles 16:9).

11

Miracles at Moriahhof

I returned to Los Angeles still in a little bit of disbelief that I had actually finished my mission in Vienna. God was very, very good to me through the whole experience there. How many impossible doors did He open up, and how many people encouraged and helped me, and how many times was my soul refreshed in the nearby Wienerwald? Dr. Loader was perhaps one in a thousand who would have put the effort and forbearance and compassion into my situation and go the extra mile to see me through while scholastically holding my feet to the fire. And all my socio-economic needs had been met and more. In view of all this, I came back giving heartfelt thanks to the Lord for His real-life demonstration that "nothing is impossible with God," even for an intellectually so-so cutthroat trout like me.

Friendly Bob and his wife, Teri, graciously offered me a room at their home in Bellflower (just south of LA) where I could dwell while I figured out what to do next. Because of activities at church, catchup socializing with Tom and Glenda, visits to and trips with Mom and Jack (we went on a wonderful Panama Canal cruise), and indecision regarding what should come next, I ended up staying put for about a year and a half. During that time, Bob and I would do a Bible study and prayer time before the sun came up, then he'd head off to his painting jobs, and I would do whatever. Maybe I should have applied to many schools of all sorts for a job—including Christian high schools and secular community colleges—but, as I mentioned before, I felt like there my unique abilities would be stifled, and in any case much of what I'd be teaching could be taught by others.

There was one more issue for me: By this time, I had developed somewhat of a mild revulsion in regard to the whole scholarly scene, especially regarding the secular academy (i.e., the part of the academy that assumes the naturalistic basis), but even a tad regarding the Christian academy. The latter could be seen in subtle ways to imitate the former. To *imitate*, for example, meant, among other things, to become mass information acquiring and disseminating machines—performing the latter through prodigious publication output that resulted in resumes that seemed to have no end. In this, Christian scholars believe that their massive written output is a search for truth, but they cannot see that in some cases pride lies behind it, and in any case it is a partial and mostly inadvertent imitation of the secular (godless) academy in which the written dissemination is ever ongoing because *truth* is something to search for but, necessarily, will never be found. To say this another way, the secular scholarly endeavor is not a means to an end (the truth) but an end in itself. The *search* and not the *find* (eureka!) is what matters, being the only thing possible. Thus he who searches the most is the greatest and most powerful scholar, not he who finds objective truth. He who searches the most gives evidence of this—and gains rank and reputation as a result—by publishing prodigiously.

But you might ask, *Then why do it at all?* Because there is prestige and power in it. As was said long ago (1 Corinthians 8:1; Proverbs 24:5), "Knowledge puffs up" and "a man of knowledge increases power." Look at today: Why do these atheistic scholars at Harvard, Yale, and Princeton have the power to push our nation in very short order from, for example, Christianity to secular humanism, free enterprise to socialism, marriage the way it's always been to marriage the way it's never been, patriarchy to matriarchy, and protecting children to killing them in the womb and cutting off their genitals once outside the womb? Because the goalless and never-ending search has caused them to run after "many schemes" (Ecclesiastes 7:29), and the next step up the ladder of pride, power, and prestige is to get (by force if necessary) the unenlightened masses to praise them for these schemes and live by them. We all want, at least a little bit, to be influential and respected, but with the secular scholars, this normal desire gets out of whack because they have no fear of God, nor of His final judgment, and because they subscribe to the "survival of the fittest" evolutionary paradigm. The upshot is that some Christian scholars may compromise a bit here and there (like I did) because they desire to have a little bit of that prominence that secular scholars seem to have. For some reason, God made me aware of this phenomenon while I was in Austria, and this in turn gave me just enough distaste for the whole academic/scholarly scene that I decided to take my *Dr. theol.* (that's how the Germans/ Austrians abbreviate it) and do some semi-scholarly things from the fringes of it.

In consideration of all this, I decided to simply find a quiet place and spend some years serving a nearby church and writing a few books concerning subjects that I cared about. So over several months at the end of 2011, I looked for a house remote enough to have peace and quiet but still within reach of my Long Beach friends. Through some providential circumstances, I found a house for sale on the northern slope of the San Bernardino mountains, a thousand feet above the valley floor with an awesome view, and bought it while the real estate market was still depressed. The evening (February 2, 2012) I picked up the keys for the house from the previous owner, Mrs. Mary Gray, and her (and my) superb real estate agent, Mrs. Karen Sanchez, my old Navy pal from training days, Mark Sommerfield, was there for the ceremony. After receiving the keys, we celebrated with a slice or two of pizza and prayed that the place would be a blessing.

That was twelve years ago, and indeed, "Moriahhof" (my pet name for the property) has been a big blessing. Because this book has already run too many pages, it seems best to now hurry through the blessings of the last decade-plus. Generally speaking, I've done as I planned, but it has been more work and mental struggle than I expected. Three areas of activity have occupied my life. They are home, my writing mission, and my church ministry. A word about each in turn.

The house itself has turned out to be near bulletproof. Being my first owned house, I worried about maintenance and cost of ownership. But both of those have really been no stress at all. Early on I tried to get to know neighbors and be hospitable, but problems arose (a few of them mind blowing), and I got the feeling after awhile that the Lord just wanted me to focus on the research and writing (and church too) and not worry about local social engagements. It's been almost supernatural how people who live in the area have let me have my "peace and quiet."

On the other hand, it seemed to be the Lord's will that I not be completely alone. Thus dogs that have had a hard life elsewhere have drifted into my domain and turned out to be wonderful daily friends. First, there was Slappy who wandered my way after he'd been shot, poisoned, and lastly, torn badly by another dog. Each time I'd nurse him back to health and send him home. But after the last visit to Dr. Engleman, he decided to stay. He was from an Aussie shepherd background it seemed, was loyal and obedient, and absolutely loved to ride anywhere anytime.

Then there was Peaches and Pepper who showed up about the time Slappy started to decline. An alcoholic man in the area had one day, while probably under the influence, adopted them from someone who had an unwanted litter. I immediately saw the handwriting on the wall, and sure enough, within a year they had both adopted me as their owner and provider. After Slappy died, the three of us carried on, and it was a three-ring circus. They protected me on my long walks through the nearby hills, and I assisted them in their jackrabbit and squirrel hunting. They loved to play "you're it!" and sometimes they'd knock me clean off my feet in the process.

After a few years, sadly, Pepper up and died suddenly, and Peaches and I carried on till just recently when she, to my dismay, came down with bad cancer and died not long after. Being just the two of us up here for several years, we had a special bond that was almost human-like in many ways. She loved me greatly, and she was at her happiest when I showed her that I loved her too. When I got the bad news from the vet about the cancer, I prayed earnestly to God that He would take her quickly when the time came and not let her nor me suffer. Soon after I took her on a special Mojave campout where we shared a BBQ meal by the campfire, then bedded down under the billion stars of the Milky Way. Several times in the cold night she bolted off in the dark to chase away some critter. On the way back we split an In-n-Out burger in Barstow. A few days later, she was unusually affectionate during the day, and then as we did our usual evening walk, she let out a cry and died. Given our decade-long relationship, how things had gone the last couple weeks, and my prayer, I felt I was kneeling on holy ground.

Ninety percent of my time at Moriahhof has been spent at my desk, reading, researching, thinking, writing, and editing. When I can't take it anymore, I have from time to time donned my boots and chest protector and helmet, fired up my old KTM (which, by the way, was made not far from Vienna), rode out of my garage, and within a few minutes accessed the nearby mountains. Along the trails are all kinds of beautiful vistas, challenging hill climbs, awesome rock formations, and incredible wildflower displays in the spring. The trails eventually connect with forest service roads that proceed on in the direction of Big Bear. Typically I'd ride the various trails ending at Coyote Flats, have a pre-packaged tuna snack at some big rocks at the top of Grapevine Canyon, doze off for a little while, coast the bike all the way down to the valley (about twenty-five minutes), then head back home along the powerline road. On special occasions, I'd treat myself to a ride down to The Depot on the western edge of Lucerne Valley (the hospitable Dave and Laura Mount, proprietors) and have me a "Depotburger" and fries. Occasionally my friend Debra Ivins (her father had years before been the long-term pastor of the church in Lucerne Valley) would meet me there to share a meal and fellowship.

My mission since arriving here has mainly been the books. So far there have been three of them, and this autobiography will be the fourth and probably the last. I'm not real motivated to do more. "The writing of many books is endless, and excessive devotion to books is wearying to the body," as Solomon said (Ecclesiastes 12:12). I initially began this vocation at an upstairs big wooden desk, but when a schizophrenic neighbor became unstable, I made my new desk a fold-up plastic table between the kitchen and the living room where I could keep a watch outside—and I have been there ever since (about nine years).

My first book was *The Slaves of Immanuel Kant*, which is about the German philosophy that finally prompted colleges and universities in America to throw their Christian faith overboard. Trying to figure out Kant's philosophy was extremely difficult, and I nearly gave up on the project multiple times. But just when I was ready to throw in the towel, I would get something that almost felt like direct inspiration from the Lord and have enough of an ah-ha moment that I could carry on with the project. Because of perplexing and grinding uncertainty about how to get published, I ended up just sitting on this book and started work on a second, *The Divine Messiah of the Tanakh*. This book shows how the Tanakh (what Jews call their Bible, which is the Christian Old Testament) strongly indicates in many ways that the coming Messiah would be the son of David *and* the Son of God—and thus divine. And again because of publishing uncertainty, I sat on that one too and began a third, *Kindness Towards Israel*. This book makes the case that the church does not completely *replace* Israel. God will fulfill His promises and prophecies made to Israel literally, and He will fulfill them figuratively (spiritually) in the church. In other words, God still has a plan for the people and land of Israel.

So there you have my scholarly literary output that I can put on my one-page CV! The three books have now been published by a family-owned publisher in Tennessee called Innovo Publishing. They have been great to work with and have given me lots of personal attention. God's provision in all this has been evident.

The first church that I went to up here was Calvary Bible Church in Lucerne Valley, about a forty-minute drive away. At that time they did not have a pastor, so I filled in where I felt I could. The brothers and sisters there were very good to me and even let me bring Slappy along when I taught the Wednesday evening Bible study (Slappy would sleep on a bed in the foyer). Right from the start, an older couple, Mr. Nick Geiger and his wife, Donna, took me under their wing and became wonderful and hospitable friends. Both Nick and Donna had worked many years for Douglas Aircraft Corporation building jetliners. When they met, Nick was a shift supervisor putting together DC-8 wings, and Donna was a "bucker" (holding the backstop for the riveter who was on the other side of the pieces of sheet metal being joined). But they didn't get married until many years later. Nick and Donna were my "high desert Tom and Glenda." On countless occasions in their sunny kitchen, we'd sip coffee and fellowship while watching the quail and roadrunners and jackrabbits come and go just outside the window. How good they were to me! Earlier in their marriage they had often gone to the Sierras to camp and fish. So between that theme and airplanes and church, we always had much to talk about. For about four or five years, they'd have me over nearly every Saturday evening where Donna would have dinner ready, then we'd talk and sip coffee or coco till late, then go to bed. I slept so good in that back guest room. Then we'd arise, have some cereal or mush, and head to church. Those were some wonderful days.

Those Saturday evenings at the Geiger's continued even though I decided after a couple years to attend a different church. There was a little "thorn" that bothered me at the Lucerne Valley church that I couldn't get solved, so it seemed better to hang my hat at Temple Baptist Church in Hesperia where I had been going for quite some time to their evening service. I have been there ever since as the unofficial, and then official, assistant pastor. I had entertained the idea of becoming the pastor of the Lucerne Valley church, but between the little "thorn" and what appeared like the Lord telling me to concentrate on my books, the shift to Hesperia seemed justified and in fact has worked out well now for many years. Still, I kept up my friendship and Saturday evening overnights with Nick and Donna as long as possible. They are both now with the Lord in glory, and I will see them again one day "soon and very soon."

I should also mention Mrs. Mary Ann Norris of Lucerne Valley who graciously offered me warm quarters at one of her Sundowner Ranch cabins when a deranged man living near my home made it impossible to stay there over the winter.

At Temple Baptist, I continue on with my "Hesperia Nick and Donna"—that is, with my dear friends Pastor Randy Burk and his blessed wife, Sandy, who have been a surrogate family, caring for me through both good times and bad. I have been Randy's "wingman" now for about eight years, and it has been a joy to serve him and the flock of the church.

My dear mother has now been freed from this difficult earthly life (d. 2021). She died at her beloved Kanati Falls Ranch in the presence of Mark and Katherine as well as her long-time assistant Miss Sharon Rawson. American Airlines graciously flew her remains back to Washington DC, and there after a brief graveside service she was laid to rest next to Dad at Arlington National Cemetery.

12

Final Thoughts

G od has been very good to me. His patience and forbearance regarding me have been great. All along as I was writing this, I had mixed feelings about publishing it. Some notable Christians in their biographies, whether self-written or not, appear to have scrupulous moral behavior and industrious character from beginning to end, and they are a great light to us all. My past was, as has been documented in this book, a mix of bad and some good from the start till the present moment, although I think with a movement toward the good after my conversion. So as I wrote the book, I didn't know if I'd do more harm than good by publishing it. Figuring that some godly counsel would help, I asked a couple deeply trusted friends to look it over and let me know their thoughts on this question. They gave their approval but only after significant changes were made.

There was some light before I got right with God. I was obedient enough to my parents to leave home with some ethics and industry, and I obeyed enough of the orders given to me in college and the Navy to have some degree of success there. In fact, in the Navy, while on the Carl Vinson, I was on the tip of the American sword for three years. If a major war had broken out during that time, I would have been in harm's way for sure, and I'm reasonably confident that I would have honorably done my duty.

But there was darkness too. As an adolescent I shook my fist at God. In my teen years I disrespected my parents badly on a few occasions, and after I flew the coop, there were instances of drunken stupidity, sexual immorality, and one or two evil things that I've decided not to mention. Because of this, I, in the eyes of the eternal and infinitely holy God, deserved death, and worse. Like on earth, as it is in heaven, any good we might do does not cancel out a crime. One can be a saint, yet one murder will make him a murderer in the eyes of man and God.

After repenting and accepting Christ at the Shamrock Ranch thirty-three years ago, there were a couple years of duplicity to come, but I soon put aside the more grievous evils that hurt me and others. The struggle against the flesh, however, will go on until the cessation of this "mortal coil."

But "with the LORD there is mercy" (Psalm 130:7). For "while we were yet sinners, Christ died for us" (Romans 5:8). I'm sixty-five now and have been around long enough and experienced enough to see firsthand the grace and mercy of God. He could have removed me from this world when I first shook my fist at Him, but He didn't. He could have done the same at the point of any of those other sins, but He didn't. Why not? Now that I know more of the Bible, I can venture a simple answer: because "God is love" and because He knew that I would submit to Him at the age of thirty-two—and so, He preserved me at least till then. Consider what Christ's disciple Peter said: "The Lord is . . . not wishing for any to perish but for all to come to repentance" (2 Peter 3:9). God did not want me to *perish*, so He kept me safe through childhood and the dangerous years of naval aviation. If a man will at some point repent and accept Christ, then God will make sure that the man lives until he has done so.

Ultimately, though, "who has known the mind of the Lord, or who [is] His counselor?" (Romans 11:34). "For as the heavens are higher than the earth," said God to the prophet Isaiah, "so are My ways higher than your ways" (Isaiah 55:9). Regarding our fate before God, it's finally His decision according to His infinite wisdom, knowledge, holiness, and love. The buck stops there. "For He says to Moses, 'I will have mercy on whom I have mercy, and I will have compassion on whom I have compassion'" (Romans 9:15). Yet, that being said, the Lord has declared clearly to us mortal men: "The one who comes to Me I will certainly not cast out" (John 6:37). Thus we are commanded by God's holy Word to "Seek!" "Come!" "Repent!" "Choose!"—"before the days of trouble come" and it is too late. If we choose wrong, it's our own fault; if we choose right, it's only by God's grace.

One thing I know for sure is that God has given me an excellent and enjoyable and exiting life, the challenges and fears and disappointments notwithstanding. He fulfilled my desire to be a fighter pilot, and now He has me in His service as a Christian pastor. The cutthroat has become a rainbow—"for nothing will be impossible with God" (Luke 1:37). This book has recorded much about adventures and achievements, but the greatest blessing has been the people who loved me along the way and especially those who added to my life a little bit more truth so that one day I'd turn my life over to God. Among these were CAPT and Mrs. Christian Engleman (my father and mother), Mrs. Connie Lehr (my Sunday school teacher), Mrs. Violet Levin, Mrs. Mary Kate Watkins, Mr. and Mrs. William Hatcher, CDR Leonard Fox, CDR Brick Immerman, and especially CAPT Eric Tibbets.

Finally this: What they taught me, is it true? Or am I and they to "be pitied" for our gullibility? When I review my life, I know that it can't be an accident. If there were no God, nothing would exist. Even if something did exist, it wouldn't be what we have here. If anything, I would be a minuscule clump of bacteria on an asteroid utterly alone in the black abyss of space. There would be no reason, no purpose, no final meaning, no life, and no love. How could there be if everything comes from nothing? On the other hand, if God does exist, then we would expect to find a world that has His creative ability and life and purpose and love all through it. So which world do we in fact have? Well, when I survey my life, it is obvious to me that there is a loving God who made it all. But each man must decide for himself. I hope, dear reader, that what you have read here will move you, even just a little bit, to see that God is and that He is calling you to be reconciled to Him through faith in His Son, Jesus Christ. "For God so loved the world, that He gave His only begotten Son, that whoever believes in Him shall not perish, but have eternal life" (John 3:16).

The End

MORE FROM
ERIC ENGLEMAN
& INNOVO PUBLISHING

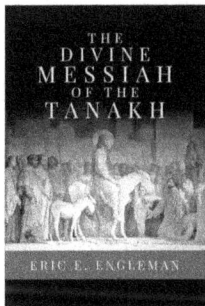

The Divine Messiah of the Tanakh

Does the Tanakh (the "Old Testament") teach the divinity of the Messiah (the Christ)? The answer is "yes!" and this book will show how.

The development of the Messiah theme in the Tanakh is a subtle progressive revelation, but there is nevertheless plenty there to demonstrate that a great king will one day come who will reconcile Jews and Gentiles back to God and will rule the earth as not only the son of David but also as the Son of God. To our natural minds, this seems impossible: the infinite God coming to us as finite man; "but with God all things are possible."

Whether you are Jew or Gentile, you will be encouraged when you learn that the king and redeemer of mankind, who will rule forever on David's throne, will not be a flawed mortal man, but the righteous eternal God.

"For a child will be born to us, a son will be given to us; And the government will rest on His shoulders; And His name will be called Wonderful Counselor, Mighty God, Eternal Father, Prince of Peace." —Isaiah 9:6

Kindness Towards Israel

Are the Old Testament's messianic-era prophecies fulfilled in the Church? Yes! Are these same prophecies fulfilled in Israel? Yes!

The Church does not completely "replace" Israel. How can this be? Because Israel fulfills these prophecies *literally*, and the Church fulfills them *spiritually* (figuratively). Through her long history, the Church has generally assumed that these prophecies describe the final, immortal, blessed ("saved") state, and thus can only be spiritually fulfilled in the Church. But, as *Kindness Towards Israel* will show, there is no clear mention in these prophecies of eternal life, and so, they rightly should find *literal* fulfillment in an earthly and temporal Israel that is separate from the Church.

Yet, based on New Testament teaching and what the Old Testament allows, these prophecies should also find *spiritual* fulfillment in a heavenly eternal Church—separate from Israel—in which *"there is neither Jew nor Greek ... for [they] are all one in Christ Jesus"* (Galatians 3:28).

The Slaves of Immanuel Kant

Did you know that the first colleges of America were all Christian colleges that prepared their students not only for this life but for the eternal life to come? Sadly, these schools today are effectively atheistic.

How did this change happen, and was it justified? As this book explains, it was largely due to the onslaught of naturalism-based science during the 1800s *as energized* by the critical philosophy of Immanuel Kant. Science pressured the schools, but the addition of Kant's super-subjectivism turned science into a religion that could not live at peace with Christianity.

In *The Slaves of Immanuel Kant*, Dr. Engleman first serves up a brief history of philosophy leading to the Enlightenment and Kant's *Critique of Pure Reason*. He refutes Kant's critical philosophy by revealing its self-refuting, circular, and even nonsensical nature. Highlighting the Christian characteristic of three sample early colleges—Harvard, Yale, and Princeton—Engleman reveals how the Kant-energized religion of science aggressively drove the old faith out of the schools in the late 1800s. The result has been a disaster, both temporally and eternally. What remains is a call for American schools to regain an eternal perspective—a perspective most excellently expressed by a great Harvard man nearly four centuries ago:

"Let every student be plainly instructed, and earnestly pressed to consider well, the main end of his life and studies is, to know God and Jesus Christ, which is eternal life, and therefore to lay Christ at the bottom, as the only foundation of all sound knowledge and learning."
—Henry Dunster, President of Harvard College 1640–1654